Emblem and motto of the Detroit Light Guard. Drawn by Frank E. Storer from the cover of the Thirty-fifth anniversary booklet by VanLeyen Company, Detroit. (Courtesy of the Frank E. Storer Collection.)

Stanley D. Solvick

LET THE DRUM BEAT

A History of the Detroit Light Guard

Wayne State University Press, Detroit, 1988

92 91 90 89 88   5 4 3 2 1

Library of Congress Cataloging-in-Publication Data

Solvick, Stanley D., 1930–
    Let the drum beat: a history of the Detroit Light Guard / Stanley
D. Solvick.
        p. cm. — (Great Lakes books)
    Bibliography: p.
    Includes index.
    ISBN 0-8143-1886-X (alk. paper)
    1. Michigan. National Guard. Infantry, 225th. Battalion, 1st—
History. 2. Detroit (Mich.)—History, Military.   I. Title.
II. Title: Detroit Light Guard.   III. Series.
UA264 225th.S65 1988
356'.1—dc19
                                                    87-34634
                                                       CIP

Special thanks is given to Lieutenant Colonel (Ret.) Frank E.
Storer for assembling the photographs and for providing the
information used in the captions.

o the officers and enlisted men of
The Detroit Light Guard,
who loyally served
their state and nation
with honor and distinction,
this volume is gratefully dedicated.

CONTENTS

Contents

ILLUSTRATIONS

ACKNOWLEDGMENTS

I particularly wish to thank the members of the History Committee of the Detroit Armory Corporation for their support and encouragement: Lieutenant Colonel James F. Clark, chairman of the committee; Lieutenant Colonel Sylvin J. Gaynor, president of the Detroit Armory Corporation; Chief Warrant Officer 4 Alfred Wyborski, its secretary; Lieutenant Colonel Frank E. Storer, who also provided the volume's illustrations and preserved many important source materials for the Light Guard; Captain Alan A. Redner; and Captain Walter R. Cyrus. I also wish to express appreciation to Lieutenant Colonel John D. McDaniels, whose dedicated chronology, "History of the Detroit Light Guard, 1708–1854" (Detroit, 1965), provided such a helpful introduction to the subject. Lieutenant Colonel McDaniels was most generous in conversations with me in sharing the results of many years of investigation.

Many archives and libraries provided much aid in the research for this work. The Burton Historical Collection of the Detroit Public Library was especially valuable, and I am particularly grateful to Mrs. Alice C. Dalligan, its chief, Mr. Joseph F. Oldenburg, its former curator of manuscripts, as well as the other members of the staff. David J. Johnson and LeRoy Barnett of the State Archives of Michigan and Richard J. Hathaway of the Library of Michigan also provided knowledgeable and sympathetic aid as did many individuals in the Public Archives of Canada, the National Archives of the United States, the libraries of the University of Michigan, and the Purdy Library of Wayne State University.

My colleague Professor Philip P. Mason provided much patient and gracious counsel and made available to me his impressive knowledge of the sources of Michigan history. Professor Sandra

15

F. VanBurkleo offered many insights into the nature of history, and Dr. Ronald E. Trunsky's unfailing good humor helped keep the problems of writing in perspective. Professor Sidney Fine has always provided guidance by serving as a model of the highest standards of scholarship.

My wife, Shirley B. Solvick, supplied continual encouragement and cheerfully volunteered much time and talent in helping me type and edit this manuscript. My parents, Pearl and Max Solvick, gave me lifelong devoted support.

INTRODUCTION

The militia had its roots in Anglo-Saxon England. Even after the conquest of that country by the Normans following the Battle of Hastings in 1066, the institution persisted and adapted itself to the new conditions. It became the obligation for all free males to serve in groups called "trained bands." The designation eventually was simplified into "train bands."[1]

Such groups of "citizen-warriors" primarily constituted defensive forces for their communities rather than a source of troops for overseas campaigns. In America, according to Richard Stone, "the first English settlers . . . brought with them an ancient militia tradition which had evolved from the Anglo-Saxon *fyrd* of Alfred the Great, Henry II's Assize of Arms (1181), Edward I's Statute of Westminster (1285), and Elizabeth I's Instructions for General Musters (1572)."[2] Given the great distance of the early settlements from the mother country and the perilous circumstances of their existence, they inevitably had to utilize citizen-soldiers drawn from their own population to supplement the small force of regular British troops in the New World. On the eve of the War for Independence each of the thirteen colonies had its own distinctive military system, but there were enough similarities in the colonial militias so that some generalizations may be made about them. Common characteristics of these systems included compulsory service, often for males whose ages ranged from sixteen to sixty. In Massachusetts for part of the seventeenth century, however, boys as young as ten had to undergo some military training. In the early period the citizen-soldiers provided protection for their communities from raids by other Europeans or hostile Indians.[3]

Eventually the colonists decided to develop troops capable of carrying a struggle into the territory of their enemy. Consequently, special forces had to be created from the regular or ordinary militia because these more comprehensive groups often included individuals too young or old or inadequately trained to possess the endurance and skill required in offensive warfare. This in turn led to the development of elite units of men particularly fit and well prepared to wage successful attacks far from their homes. These individuals were usually volunteers, thus creating the distinction between volunteer or independent militia and the regular or ordinary militia.[4]

The former led to the proud American practice of the volunteer military company, which in the twentieth century became absorbed into the United States National Guard. The Detroit Light Guard, the city's oldest militia unit, stems from this special heritage. This study, a history of the group, utilizes all the available source materials to present its story to contemporary and future generations of volunteers who will carry on the tradition.

Notes

1. Lyle D. Brundage, "The Organization, Administration, and Training of the United States Ordinary and Volunteer Militia, 1792–1861" (Ed.D. diss., University of Michigan, 1958), 1.

2. Darrett B. Rutman, *A Militant New World, 1607–1640* (1959; reprint, New York, 1979), 10–15; Richard G. Stone, Jr., *A Brittle Sword: The Kentucky Militia, 1776–1912* (Lexington, Ky., 1977), 1–2.

3. John M. Palmer, *America in Arms* (1941; reprint, New York, 1979), 17; Brundage, 2–4.

4. J. Palmer, 16–18. John K. Mahon, *History of the Militia and the National Guard* (New York, 1983), contains the best accounts of the militia and National Guard from the perspective of a contemporary scholar.

1

Origins of the Detroit Militia

Detroit was established as a western outpost of New France on 24 July 1701 by an expedition led by Antoine de la Mothe Cadillac. This force had departed from Montreal early two months before, having been authorized at the highest levels of the royal government. The new colony had a variety of purposes. One was to block British expansion in the area of the straits, or "Le Detroit," as the French called the entire series of waterways between Lakes Erie and Huron, including the Detroit River. The settlement also was meant to become a center of the fur trade, where farming would be practiced as well. Another intention was to both protect and control friendly Indians by concentrating a large number of them near this new citadel of Gallic military power. Given its isolated location, Cadillac's town, which he tactfully named "Fort Pontchartrain du Detroit," after his leading patron at the royal court at Versailles, had

to be concerned with defense. Indeed, half of the first one hundred settlers of the outpost were professional soldiers. The location of the colony, now near the foot of Woodward Avenue at the Detroit River, had been chosen by the French because the river banks at that time rose to a height of forty feet above the water level. A small river, the Savoyard, later diverted into the sewers beneath the town, ran at a diagonal behind the bluff where the settlers landed and emptied into the Detroit River. Thus Cadillac's village from the first occupied a position with a good military advantage.[1]

Fort Pontchartrain du Detroit's garrison always contained a small number of regular soldiers, so the members of the militia played an integral role in assuring the safety of the community. A good many of the local habitants, as the French colonists in the New World were often called, had military experience. Cadillac, himself a professional soldier, made an especial effort to recruit as settlers troops who had been assigned to protect Fort Pontchartrain. Such men ought to receive grants of land, he felt, because in addition to following civilian pursuits their martial background would make them able members of the community's militia. The French king gave Cadillac permission to award such grants.[2]

The French rule at Fort Pontchartrain ended after nearly sixty years when, at the cessation of the fighting in the French and Indian War in the fall of 1760, English forces arrived to assume control of the area which would in the future become Michigan. A peace treaty between Great Britain and France signed three years later formalized this change of hands. During the period of English rule at Detroit, the anglicized version of the Gallic name, the practice of having only a modest garrison was continued. Consequently, the safety of the community required maintaining the militia, and both French- and English-speaking citizens served in it. This became especially important in 1763, when a series of anti-British Indian insurrections swept across North America. During the hostilities at Detroit, known as Pontiac's Rebellion, the post successfully repelled the attacks of a coalition of tribes led by the intrepid and wily Chief Pontiac. The British troops were victorious not only because they were commanded by a particularly able and determined officer, Major Henry Gladwin, but also because the English had the support of the local militia.[3]

During the American War for Independence Detroit and the surrounding territory remained loyal to the Crown. Since the area had only recently been acquired by the British, most of the population of European origin consisted of Frenchmen. These habitants had no particular desire to aid members of the thirteen original colonies in their fight to preserve what they regarded as their constitutional rights as Englishmen. The small British group in Michigan was made up largely of merchants dependent on the protection of the royal army. The powerful Indian tribes of this region had become reconciled to English rule by 1776 and regarded the Crown as their protector against land-hungry colonists from the East Coast. The treaty of 1783, which formally concluded the revolutionary war, awarded the area now encompassing Michigan to the United States of America. Due to a number of unresolved disputes between Great Britain and the United States and the fact that English officials in the New World highly valued the military and commercial importance of the upper Great Lakes region, British forces did not withdraw from the area into Canada until the summer of 1796. The Stars and Stripes finally replaced the Union Jack in Detroit at noon on 11 July.[4]

Michigan began its history as a section of the United States as part of the Northwest Territory, which had been created by Congress in 1787. Since the centers of European population were relatively few in that region of the country, huge counties were created around those settlements which did exist. Consequently, Winthrop Sargent, secretary of the Northwest Territory, who was serving as acting governor in August 1796, proclaimed a county with Detroit as its center of government. The subdivision included most of the present state of Michigan and healthy slices of Ohio, Indiana, Wisconsin, and even the corner of Illinois that now contains Chicago. The county was named

"Wayne" after Mad Anthony Wayne, commander of the United States Army in its notable victory over the Indian allies of the British at the Battle of Fallen Timbers in August 1794.[5]

The American officials took over and strengthened the existing militia organization of Detroit. "Under the earliest laws of the Northwest Territory all male citizens, between the ages of sixteen and fifty years, were enrolled in companies, and required to parade for two hours every Saturday in the year. Whenever persons so enrolled assembled for public worship, they were required to go fully armed and equipped, or be subject to a fine. No provision was made for a uniform of any kind, and there was little need of any." The presumption was that if a citizen could shoot straight, "the question as to whether he wore a blue coat, or any coat at all, was of but little moment." Within a few years the territorial militia laws were altered to specify that "all persons over eighteen and under forty-five were to be enrolled, and to provide their own guns, ammunition, and accoutrements."[6]

In the early years of the new republic, the militia bolstered the security of Detroit, particularly because there had been a "gradual decay of the Fort and the stockade under the continuous barrage of . . . time and weather." The militia played an important role in the life of Detroit. In the area that still contained a preponderantly French society, the citizen-soldiers joined in the celebrations associated with Mardi Gras. The organization helped provide coherence and cohesion to the small community as well as furnishing protection for it. In the February 1800 funeral observances for George Washington, who had died in December of the previous year, members of the militia joined a contingent of the regular army from the fort and citizens of the area to make up a "funeral cortege 'which exceeded any thing of the Kind ever seen at this Place.'"[7]

Detroit in the first decades of the nineteenth century was a relatively peaceful community that had no professional police force, although one individual was appointed to serve as a peace officer and to perform some clerical duties. Homicide was rare in the area, but on one occasion a native American warrior called Kish-ku-kon, also known as "the Chippeway Rogue," had been charged with murder. Local officials, fearful that the prisoner might escape from the inadequate jail, requested Colonel François Chabert to provide "a detail of militia as a guard until the prison should be rebuilt."[8]

In 1803, when Ohio became the first state to be carved out of the Old Northwest, Michigan for a time was part of the Indiana Territory. Detroiters felt, however, that they deserved to belong to a separate entity. They repeatedly petitioned Congress, and finally a bill passed the national legislature and was signed by President Jefferson in early 1805 that provided for a separate Michigan Territory as of 1 July 1805. The first governor of Michigan was to be William Hull, a Connecticut-born, Yale-trained lawyer and politician who had settled in Massachusetts and became an ardent supporter of Jefferson. Michigan required an executive with a sophisticated knowledge of military affairs. The territory was part of an isolated frontier peopled by many fierce and independent-minded Indian tribes still not reconciled to the departure of their British friends or the rule of the United States, which the native Americans associated with land-hungry white settlers. Most United States citizens also expected a second conflict with England, and Michigan's shared border with Canada emphasized the need for a governor who could provide military leadership. Hull seemed to be such an individual. He had been trained as a colonial militia officer and during the War for Independence "had seen service in thirteen battles, had led several bayonet charges, had been cited twice for bravery, and had been promoted to the rank of lieutenant-colonel in the regulars." After the end of the American Revolution, Hull continued for a time as an officer in the regular army before he resigned to follow civilian pursuits. Even then, he remained a commander of a Massachusetts militia division.[9]

Despite his impressive military background, however, Hull proved to be a very poor choice for governor of Michigan. He had no sense of the needs of frontier settlers. Although he had experience in public affairs in Massachusetts and had been elected to its legislature as well as serving as a judge in that state, Hull demonstrated a lamentably poor political sense in dealing with both the people of Michigan and his colleagues in the territorial government. He took himself as well as his duties exceedingly seriously. He failed to make the necessary effort to understand the frontier population with whom he had to deal and never established a rapport with the settlers. Such problems affected his command of the citizen-soldiers of the territory.[10]

Actually, Hull's leadership displayed both his strengths and weaknesses as a governor. He gave Michigan's military forces the highest priority in his administration. The chief executive as well

as the judges appointed to serve the area comprised a legislative council for the territory under congressional statute. Only four days after the new government began to function, "the Governor and Judges convened. . . . On the motion of the Governor [they] resolved that a committee be appointed to take into consideration the organization of the Militia of the Territory of Michigan and report thereon to this body."[11]

By the end of that August the Michigan Militia Act had been approved as part of the Woodward Code of 1805. The law provided for the establishment of the territory's force of citizen-soldiers: "Compulsory enrollment was required of free, able-bodied males from ages fourteen to fifty. The commander-in-chief was authorized to organize the militia, provide for uniforms, appoint officers, set training or muster days, appoint courts martial, and conduct routine activities." Since the governor was the head of the Michigan military, Hull was able to give full rein to his ideas about the way the citizen-soldiers should be organized. In September he issued orders that Michigan would have two regiments of the regular, or ordinary, militia, consisting of recruits discharging their required service. Hull divided Michigan into four districts: Detroit, Huron, Michilimackinac, and Erie. The First Regiment would encompass men from the first three districts, with the Second Regiment including those from the last. In addition, there would be a special Legionary Corps, consisting of volunteers only. This body began the tradition of the independent militia company in Michigan and, thus, is the precursor of the Detroit Light Guard.[12]

The most controversial of Hull's regulations involved the detailed and rigid specifications for the uniforms the citizen-soldiers would wear. These rules ranged from outlining the kind of yellow buttons and blue coats that generals would wear to the white buttons, white vests, and blue pantaloons of privates. Michiganians of the early 1800s, who saw the world from the frontiersman's perspective, were not persuaded that the art of war necessitated a soldier's having "the length of the coat . . . precisely to the knee." Such dress seemed unnecessary, perhaps even unmanly, to the westerner of the period. The regulation uniforms, moreover, constituted a burdensome expense to many individuals. Men of modest means already losing valuable time from work to take part in training were in no position to bear the cost of providing themselves with the governor's notion of proper military costume. Complicating the situation was the fact that much of the cloth and other items specified in the regulations for the citizen-soldier's dress were not readily available in Detroit. Hull, however, had brought a supply of the needed materials to Michigan from the East. The reaction of many of the local inhabitants was not one of gratitude. Referring to the chief executive's requirements for the Michigan militia, a local citizen observed that

the chief of the officers complied with his orders, but the soldiers, more from poverty than from contumacy, did not comply. Blue cloth could not be got at that time, in any of the stores where the people were accustomed to traffic, and they could not command money to purchase their uniforms at the Governor's shop.

The same orders were again repeated, and all the captains of companies were commanded to enforce obedience to the orders, by fine and imprisonment. By means of this bare-faced imposition, he emptied a considerable store of money out of the pockets of the people in a direct line into his own.

Such a view does not constitute a completely fair or balanced analysis of William Hull's leadership, but it does reflect a widespread perception of the governor's actions that complicated his ability to successfully command the militia. His belief in the importance of proper uniforms in the training of soldiers accorded with the military theory of the time, but the obsessive and unbending way in which he designed and applied his regulations did constitute a serious defect in his leadership.[13]

Michiganians continually complained to the federal government about Hull's actions in the territory, but their protests went unheeded in Washington. Unfortunately, the national administration also ignored the governor's consistent pleas for strengthening the defenses of the territory. Since he had assumed the direction of Michigan at a time when many informed Americans thought it likely that a second war with Great Britain would erupt within a few years, he implored federal authorities to station more regular troops at Detroit and to stockpile more munitions and related military supplies there. Above all, William Hull urged that the United States build and maintain a fleet that would control the Great Lakes in case of a struggle with England. Virtually nothing, however, was done to secure the safety of the Old Northwest until the eve of the predicted war, and even that consisted of what a later generation would call "too little and too late."[14]

In the meantime the work of organizing and maintaining the Michigan militia continued. Whatever resentments serving in the military may have caused among some citizens, the periodic parades appealed to the children of the community, who delighted in the music "of the drum and fife" as well as the gingerbread that was generously distributed on drill days. Some of the adults appear to have developed a zest for the "rough merriment always caused by certain reckless and unruly spirits." Despite tensions and differences of opinion in the community over Michigan's military policies, muster continued "every Sunday at four o'clock in the afternoon for the purpose of military exercise." On such occasions the recruits were to "be faithfully exercised for at least one hour and a half after arriving on parade, and longer, if required, until dismissed." Moreover, "every officer and soldier of the militia throughout the Territory [was] to place in their houses . . . all instruments by which they could annoy an assaulting enemy, and [was] to be in readiness to repair with their arms and ammunition in good order to any point of attack, on a short alarm."[15]

The key officers of the militia in the early years of the Michigan Territory included Colonel Augustus B. Woodward as commander of the First Regiment, Colonel John Anderson of the Second Regiment, and Lieutenant Colonel Elijah Brush of the Legionary Corps. Hull had particular trouble with the brilliant, eccentric, and abrasive Judge Woodward in the management of the citizen-soldiers. The jurist was especially critical of the company of black militia that the governor raised primarily from the ranks of slaves who had escaped from Canada, where slavery existed at that time, to the free soil of Michigan. Woodward may have been less concerned with the racial origins of these men or the legality of their presence on American soil than he was eager to use any means whatsoever to attack Hull. The former complained to the Michigan Legislative Council about the offending unit, and he was rebuffed as follows: "It is found to be true, that the Governor has given permission to the Black male Inhabitants, to exercise as a military Company, that he has appointed a Black man by the name of Peter Denison to command them. . . . It further appears . . . that they have ever conducted in an orderly manner, manifested, on all occasions, an attachment to our government, and a determination to aid in the defence of the Country, whenever their services should be required." This reply to Woodward continued, and regarding any possibility of the citizen-soldiers in question as "being slaves, the Committee only observes, that they were black persons who resided in the Territory, and were not claimed as slaves, by any person or persons in the original states." As residents of Michigan, therefore, the black militiamen were "subject to the laws, and entitled to the protection of the Government."[16]

Although Hull had his differences with his colleagues and the people he governed, they concurred with him in his disappointment in the reluctance of the federal government to prepare for a conflict. They were not much reassured by the last-minute actions Washington took to protect the area just before the outbreak of the War of 1812.[17] The War Department appointed Hull commander of its newly created Northwest Army, a large part of which consisted of relatively untrained Ohio militia. His responsibilities involved not only protecting the entire upper Great Lakes area but conducting an invasion of Canada as well. The governor reluctantly followed his instructions and crossed the Detroit River into British territory on 12 July 1812. Since the other side of the river had until 1796 been part of the same community, Hull did not take with him members of the Detroit militia in order to avoid pitting friends and relatives against each other. His foray into Canada proved to be a brief and abortive one. The American forces lacked the proper artillery to lay siege to Fort Malden at Amherstburg on the British side of the Detroit River. Hull worried about the Indian allies of the English attacking Detroit from northern Michigan and in general feared his position was too exposed. By 8 August he had withdrawn his troops back to the American side of the river.[18]

A few days later the astute British general Isaac Brock arrived at Fort Malden and demanded that Detroit surrender. This led to a short, ineffective artillery exchange across the river. Hull's defiance of the British ultimatum was just as brief. When Brock soon afterwards crossed to the United States shore, the American commander decided to surrender Detroit and its fort without a struggle. He apparently reasoned that given the English naval supremacy on the Great Lakes and the Indians' domination of the land routes to Michigan, he was isolated from any reinforcements or additional supplies. Any siege of Detroit would, thus, inevitably end in a British victory, and he feared that in such circumstances Brock would not be able to prevent his Indian allies from massacring civilians in the heat of battle. Therefore, on 16 August 1812, Hull surrendered his entire army as well as the town of Detroit to the English. Members of the Michigan militia, after turning in their weapons, were permitted to return to their homes. Similarly, the men from Ohio were allowed to go back to their native state on "parole," that is to say they gave up their guns and promised not to resume fighting unless they were first exchanged for captured English soldiers of comparable rank. The regular troops were sent as prisoners to Quebec.[19]

Detroit was occupied by the British until September 1813, when in the wake of a decisive naval victory at the Battle of Lake Erie by the American fleet commanded by Oliver Hazard Perry, United States forces drove the British from the Great Lakes area. Once freedom had been restored to Michigan, President James Madison replaced the disgraced Hull as governor of the Michigan Territory with Lewis Cass, a New Hampshire-born Ohio settler who had distinguished himself during the fighting. Cass, whose background included law, politics, and the military, proved to be one of the most distinguished chief executives in the history of Michigan.[20]

During the long period of Cass's governorship—he relinquished the office to enter Jackson's cabinet in 1831—he effectively commanded the militia while providing the leadership that brought Michigan from a sparsely settled territory to a bustling area on the eve of statehood. Although there was the usual postwar loss of interest in things military, Cass tried to emphasize the need for maintaining protection for the region. One of the first things Cass did as commander in chief of

Michigan's militia was to proclaim the reorganization of its forces: "I hereby do revoke and declare void all commissions in the Militia of the Territory, which have been issued previous to the date of this proclamation. . . . This 21st day of July, in the year of our Lord one thousand eight hundred and eighteen and of the Independence of the United States the forty-third." This dismissal of all prior commissions allowed the governor to rearrange the Wolverine military forces in more systematic fashion.[21]

Maintaining the militia, however, was not an easy task. Sometimes it proved hard to persuade citizens to undertake their martial obligations. John R. Williams, the territory's adjutant general, detailed in a report to the secretary of war the difficulties in obtaining the necessary information about the "correct . . . number and organization of the Militia." The problems in convincing citizens to turn out for muster were revealed by the announcement of S. T. Davinport, Jr., captain of the City Militia of Detroit: "I shall be in my office . . . from 12 until 4 o'clock tomorrow, to hear the excuses of those who were notified and did not attend parade on Monday last. Those who were not armed and equipped as the law directs will pay over to the orderly Sergeant twelve and a half cents for each article in which they were deficient."[22]

In the same summer the Michigan Legislative Council enacted a new militia act because it could not find the text of the original law. The organization of the territory's fighting forces, however, did not seem to be significantly altered. Cass did continue to give heavy emphasis to military matters, being acutely aware of Michigan's exposed situation. He particularly stressed the need for leadership in those in positions of authority, stating: "The militia can never be either useful, efficient, or respectable unless all officers whose duty it is to set a proper example perform their duty, with fidelity, activity, and zeal."[23]

The governor appealed to the "honor, patriotism, and duty" of everyone who served under his command, especially those who held responsible posts. As Cass eloquently stated, "It is . . . the duty and interest of every friend to this country not only to foster a military spirit but to encourage it by individual example." In particular, he praised "Captain Woodworth and the spartan band under his command, for their laudable zeal and example, this company of Artillery being the first of the militia in this territory that has appeared in uniform since the year 1812, and their fine military appearance, it is hoped, will stimulate others to their patriotic exertions. . . . Go on then American Citizen-Soldiers, in the laudable career which you have handsomely opened." Then Cass, the son of a veteran of the War for Independence who had himself carried on the family tradition in the country's second struggle with Great Britain, summarized his feelings about Michigan's armed forces: "Upon this remote and exposed frontier, the importance of arming the whole body of the militia cannot but be duly appreciated."[24]

Although the voluntary members of the Legionary Corps continued to play a key role in the militia, often turning out in complete uniform for their meetings at Woodworth's Hotel in Detroit, it often was difficult to persuade the majority of the ordinary militia to take their obligations seriously.

Maintaining an atmosphere of discipline represented a particular challenge for the territory's leaders. On some occasions it became necessary to court-martial individuals for "unofficer-like and ungentlemanly conduct," such as "not preventing fighting and rioting, when a company [was] assembled."[25]

During the 1820s the regular and volunteer militia persisted in Michigan, but in those relatively peaceful years the citizens were not so vigorous as they should have been in fulfilling their martial responsibilities. "Ours is a border country," Cass felt it necessary to emphasize, "and the lessons of experience have been too recent and too dear-bought to be speedily forgotten." Despite the decline of interest on the part of many Michiganians in maintaining their defenses, the area's leaders never forgot their country's heritage in this regard. "Among the most precious and proudest privileges of American citizens," recalled one, "is the right to keep and bear arms." It is against this background that a desire developed among civic-minded Detroiters to reorganize the volunteer militia as a reinvigorated independent company.[26]

Under the leadership of Edward Brooks, a veteran of the War of 1812, these concerned volunteer militiamen created the Detroit City Guards in 1830, a new framework for carrying on an old tradition. This unit took part in the short-lived 1832 Black Hawk War, named for a leader of the Sauk and Fox Indians who fomented a rebellion in the spring and summer of that year. The uprising began in Illinois and sent a wave of apprehension through surrounding areas. One historian observed that "not only were the inhabitants of the western frontier alarmed and fearful, but the terror spread throughout Michigan, even to Detroit." The governor of Illinois, who had mobilized his state's forces and asked for federal troops, pleaded with Stevens T. Mason, the acting governor of the Michigan Territory, for help.[27]

Responding quickly to this request, Mason authorized John R. Williams, major general in charge of the territory's militia, to assemble an appropriate expedition. Williams summoned various military forces to meet on the morning of 24 May at Conrad Ten Eyck's popular tavern located on the River Rouge. The Detroiters, including the City Guards, now led by Captain Isaac S. Rowland, began their march toward Chicago. In the meantime, however, the Illinois militia and the regular army subdued Black Hawk and his followers. Governor Mason called back most of the Michigan militia, including the City Guards, just as they marched beyond Ypsilanti. Williams and some of his staff officers, however, were ordered to proceed to Chicago where they received the thanks of the people of Illinois for Michigan's offer of help at a moment of crisis. Among the individuals who continued with Williams was Colonel Brooks, the first leader of the City Guards, so symbolically the unit was represented at the conclusion of the Black Hawk War.[28]

The next few years proved quiet ones for the City Guards. In 1836 the leaders of the local volunteer militia once again decided to reorganize. The advent of the Brady Guards provides the next chapter to Detroit's long-standing military tradition.

Notes

1. George N. Fuller, ed., *Michigan: A Centennial History of the State and Its People* (Chicago, 1939), 1:12; Milo M. Quaife and Sidney Glazer, *Michigan: From Primitive Wilderness to Industrial Commonwealth* (New York, 1948), 55–58; Silas Farmer, *History of Detroit and Wayne County and Early Michigan*, 3d ed., rev. and enl. (1890; reprint, Detroit, 1969), 3; "Cadillac Papers," *Historical Collections: Collections and Researches Made by the Michigan Pioneer and Historical Society* 33 (1904): 42–44.

2. Fuller, 1:40–44, 70; "Cadillac Papers," 137, 169–70.

3. Fuller, 1:64–68; F. Clever Bald, *Michigan in Four Centuries* (New York, 1954), 67–75; Willis F. Dunbar, *Michigan: A History of the Wolverine State*, rev. ed. George S. May (Grand Rapids, Mich., 1980), 78–85; Quaife and Glazer, 87–88; Howard H. Peckham, *Pontiac and the Indian Uprising* (Princeton, N.J., 1947), 194–204.

4. Fuller, 1:73–75; Quaife and Glazer, 100–112; Bald, *Detroit's First American Decade, 1796 to 1805*, University of Michigan Publications, History and Political Science, vol. 16 (Ann Arbor, Mich., 1948), 18–19; Dunbar, 122.

5. Fuller, 1:95–107; Quaife and Glazer, 118–20; Dunbar, 115–26.

6. Farmer, 313.

7. Bald, *Detroit*, 4, 102–3, 164.

8. Ibid., 195–96, 223–24.

9. Fuller, 1:112–14; Bald, *Michigan*, 106; Quaife and Glazer, 125; Dunbar, 135; Alec R. Gilpin, *The War of 1812 in the Old Northwest* (1958; reprint, East Lansing, Mich., 1968), 23.

10. Quaife and Glazer, 125–26; Dunbar, 135–41; Farmer, 97, 134; Gilpin, *The Territory of Michigan [1805–1837]* (East Lansing, Mich., 1970), 15–20, 31–32, 36–38.

11. Minutes of the Michigan Legislative Council, 5 July 1805, Augustus B. Woodward Papers, Burton Historical Collection, Detroit Public Library (hereafter cited as BHC).

12. Gilpin, *Territory*, 47–48; Quaife and Glazer, 129.

13. Farmer, 314–15; Dunbar, 140; Gilpin, *Territory*, 48.

14. Gilpin, *Territory*, 51–55; Gilpin, *War of 1812*, 26–28; Quaife and Glazer, 130–31; Dunbar, 147–48; Fuller, 1:124.

15. Farmer, 316; General Order, Stanley Griswold, Acting Governor, Detroit, 2 June 1806, William Woodbridge Papers, BHC.

16. Gilpin, *Territory*, 48; Resolutions to the Legislative Council, 17 Oct. 1808, Woodward Papers, BHC; "Report of the Committee to Whom Was Referred the Resolutions Presented to This Legislature," 17 Oct. 1808, Woodward Papers, BHC.

17. Dunbar, 147–48; Gilpin, *War of 1812*, 27–28; Gilpin, *Territory*, 53.

18. Fuller, 1:124–27; Quaife and Glazer, 131–34; Dunbar, 148–54.

19. Fuller, 1:127–28; Quaife and Glazer, 134–35; Dunbar, 154–56; Gilpin, *War of 1812*, 109–19.

20. Quaife and Glazer, 139–43; Bald, *Michigan*, 134–40; Dunbar, 159–61.

21. Dunbar, 222; *Detroit Gazette*, 23 July 1818.

22. General Order, John R. Williams, Attorney General, 26 Aug. 1818, Records of the Michigan Military Establishment, 1838–1941, p. 10, Michigan State Archives, Lansing (hereafter cited as MSA); *Detroit Gazette*, 9 Oct. 1818.

23. *Detroit Gazette,* 31 [23?] July 1818; John R. Williams to John C. Calhoun, 8 May 1822, Records of the Michigan Military Establishment, p. 76, MSA.

24. Williams to Calhoun, 8 May 1822, Records of the Michigan Military Establishment, p. 76, MSA; *Detroit Gazette,* 9, 22 July 1819; Gilpin, *Territory,* 63.

25. *Detroit Gazette,* 24 Dec. 1819, 4 Feb., 22 Sept. 1820.

26. Ibid., 11 June 1824; General Order, J. C. Schwarz, Adjutant General, 25 July 1831, Records of the Michigan Military Establishment, MSA.

27. United States Department of the Army, *Lineage and Honors: 225th Infantry (Detroit Light Guard)* (Washington, 1969), 1; "Your History!" *The Light Guard,* 1 (6 May 1952) 1, Collection of Lieutenant Colonel Frank E. Storer, Detroit (hereafter cited as Storer); Matilde Z. Zackem, "Michigan's Aid in the Black Hawk War," Master's thesis, Wayne State University, 1943, 14.

28. Zackem, 16–26; John Robertson, "Brief Military History of Michigan as a Territory and as a State," in Michigan Commission for the Semi-Centennial of the Admission of the State of Michigan into the Union, *Addresses Delivered at Its Celebration, June 15, 1886,* (Detroit, 1886), 459–60; Robert E. Roberts to John Robertson, 22 Feb., 4 Mar. 1882, Records Relating to the Black Hawk War, MSA.

2

From the Brady Guards to the Light Guard

In 1836 Michigan still had many of the characteristics of a western frontier state. Politically it constituted a stronghold of the Jacksonian Democrats, and Old Hickory was a hero to most Michiganians. Indeed, four years later when the people of Michigan abandoned the party of Jackson for the opposition Whigs, it was because the latter group had nominated William Henry Harrison, a popular general who had made his reputation in the Old Northwest and who still had the "'smell of gunpowder' on him."[1]

Michigan in 1836 also found itself in a curious constitutional limbo; it paradoxically had become a state that was not yet a state, its plea for admission to the union having been rebuffed by Congress at the urging of the influential Ohio delegation because the leaders of the Michigan Territory refused to withdraw its persuasive claims to the

approximately four hundred square miles of land known as the Toledo strip. Unwilling to accept the refusal from Washington, the youthful Stevens T. Mason led Michiganians in what constituted a process of do-it-yourself statehood. In 1835 Michigan established itself as a de facto state, setting up an effective government, but one which could not receive official status until Congress gave its approval. A vital prerogative of statehood is the ability to have a congressional delegation, but the Senate and the House of Representatives judge the qualifications of its members, and these bodies would not seat individuals elected by Michigan until its inhabitants gave their assent to a border settlement that would cede Toledo to Ohio. Indeed, this dispute erupted into the series of incidents known as the "Toledo War," which had occurred in the prior year. In that episode Governor Mason's heavy use of the Michigan military forces alerted Detroiters to the need for an expanded and re-organized unit of volunteer militia.[2]

The international climate also encouraged thoughtful and civic-minded individuals to seek a revitalization and continuation of the organization of citizen-soldiers in the area. The 1830s and 1840s in the United States were years of exuberant self-confidence and expansionism, traits which co-alesced into the philosophy and policy of Manifest Destiny. This feisty belief in the rightness and in-evitability of extending the borders of the United States produced strains from time to time between the young republic and Great Britain. The ever-present possibility that hostilities could resume en-couraged sentiments for a strong local self-defense force in this border area.

In the generation after the end of the War of 1812 concern about things military had de-clined, as so often happens after a major war. This was especially true of interest in the regular or ordi-nary militia, which, in contrast to volunteer com-panies, consisted of individuals compelled to serve by law. For example, the *Detroit Gazette* a few years before the reorganization of the militia into the Brady Guards had reprinted approvingly a dispatch from an eastern paper of the period that observed: "The legislature of Delaware has wholly abolished the Militia System of that State." Although the correspondent quoted affected an air of objectivity toward the citizen-soldier, the article contained a supercilious tone, for the author indicated that Delaware's actions were understandable given the reputed inefficiency that characterized the perfor-mance of the regular militia: "Great complaints are made by all the States in the Union. . . . The

soldiers, in spite of their swords and guns and all the pomp and circumstance of war, are treated with contempt and insult."[3]

The editor of the *Detroit Gazette,* respond-ing to this story shortly afterward, complained that there was too much "humbug" in the militia sys-tems of the country. Yet such harsh criticism per-tained not to the concept of the citizen-soldier as such but rather to the disorganized, poorly trained condition of these units in many parts of the United States. To many observers they seemed so ineffective that they constituted an unnecessary imposition on the schedules of the farmers, me-chanics, and shopkeepers compelled to take time off from their daily occupations to attend training. Sometimes a lack of discipline plagued the drills; in some parts of the country campaigning politicians visited units to ply the militiamen with liquor and promises, both of a dubious quality.[4]

If the ordinary militia with its unwilling recruits no longer provided an adequate answer to the country's security needs, then the modest reg-ular army would have to be supplemented by that very special and distinctive unit, the volunteer or independent militia company. It was with this in mind that a small group of men came together on Saturday evening, 2 April 1836, to reorganize De-troit's City Guards into what eventually became the Brady Guards. They met in a hall described simply as the "large room over the Museum." Rec-ords depict this gathering as "a meeting of the Young Men of the city of Detroit for the purpose of forming a volunteer Independent corps for said city."[5] During the proceedings, a public-spirited community leader, Marshal J. Bacon, briefly but eloquently explained the need for a reorganized militia unit. The group then appointed Colonel John Winder, who had chaired the meeting, to head a committee to prepare a constitution and bylaws for the proposed organization.[6]

This gathering had of course involved earlier preparation, perhaps beginning more than a year in advance. For some time individuals who had been active in the Detroit City Guards had wanted to reformulate the group into an even more professional and sophisticated volunteer unit. More than half a century after the creation of the Brady Guards, one of the men involved, Andrew T. McReynolds, recalled, "My mind often reverts to the time when Isaac S. Rowland, John Chester, Marshal J. Bacon and your humble servant met in the office of Major Rowland in the old Smart block, in the winter of 1834–5, and resolved on organizing an independent volunteer military company. . . . The young men of Detroit rallied around the little nucleus that we thus formed, resulting in the organization of the Brady Guard." McReynolds also claimed to have written the original draft of the Brady Guards' pledge.[7]

Reorganizing an existing unit, the City Guards, to form a new company involved complex and demanding efforts. The first organizational meeting was quickly followed by another on 6 April. At this second meeting the name Brady Guards was used for the first time, but the group apparently regarded 13 April as the founding date for the reorganized unit. It was at the meeting on this date that the constitution and bylaws were adopted. A clear continuity, however, exists from the 2 April meeting. At that gathering committees had been appointed to deal with practical matters ranging from a suitable uniform for the proposed

company through a constitution and bylaws to the selection of a drill officer "forthwith." So even in the early stages of the formation of the new group, the membership wished to start training immediately, in keeping with its fundamental purpose. A special committee was named to begin securing whatever appropriate supplies might be available from the federal government by corresponding "with the honorable, the Secretary of War, and obtain[ing] a requisition on the commanding officer of the United States Arsenal at Dearbornville for one hundred stand of arms, eight side arms and the necessary equipage."[8]

Every military unit has a distinctive, if not unique, character. This quality particularly typifies the voluntary militia company. These groups often choose names that reflect their special qualities or origins. The public-spirited volunteers who assembled in the large room above the museum early in April authorized a special committee to select such a designation. One individual loomed so prominently in the military affairs of Detroit in the 1830s that the real task of the committee would be not to ponder on the possible appellation of the company so much as to obtain the consent of this man to be associated with it. This individual was a soldier whose roots were entwined with the early military history of the United States. He enjoyed a long, distinguished, and colorful career, which culminated in his appointment as commander of the federal garrison at Detroit as well as of "Military Department No. 7, which meant that all the United States troops and forts in the northwest, between Detroit and the Mississippi, were under his command."[9]

This outstanding officer, General Hugh

Brady, had been born in 1768 in a hamlet called Standing Stone in Huntington County, Pennsylvania. The fifth of six sons in a family of ten children, Brady's values and pride in his country may be gleaned from his comment, "My brothers all lived to be men, in every sense of the term; and at a period when the qualities of men were put to the most severe and enduring tests."[10] Brady, one of the most fascinating of military figures in the history of Detroit, cannot be properly understood unless he is seen against the background of his time. His father, John, was a substantial farmer on the Pennsylvania frontier. In response to fierce British and Indian attacks on outlying American settlements during the War for Independence, the elder Brady took leave from his regular army regiment to return home and organize the frontiersmen into militia groups to protect themselves. During this home-front duty John Brady died from wounds received during a clash with a band of Indians. The father who had moved back and forth between regular army and citizen-soldier status with ease and who dedicated his life to his community served as a model for his son. Hugh Brady would combine a distinguished career in the regular army with a vital and constructive role in Detroit and its militia. If the elder Brady had served his country well during the War for Independence, Hugh achieved even greater distinction during America's second war with Great Britain. He attained fame as one of the heroes of the bloody battle at Lundy's Lane near Niagara Falls in 1814. If Hugh Brady had done nothing else, he would have won the admiration of his generation as well as the grudging respect of the British for his role in the War of 1812.[11]

Despite his achievements and prestige, Brady always maintained a dry, self-deprecatory wit, which further endeared him to those he knew. After the revolutionary war he had experimented with several civilian occupations but developed enthusiasm for none of them. He decided to refresh himself and regain a sense of perspective and a feeling for roots by returning to his family for an extended visit. He later recalled of this time, "I became weary of an idle life and began to look for my promised fortune; but, up to this day, have never been able to find it." This statement contained more of Brady's humor than his usual accuracy, for he soon left his family to rejoin the United States Army and went on to achieve a richly distinguished career. Military service seemed to Brady the most natural and appropriate vocation to follow. He liked to point out that "the Government has provided for me. I have returned her some service, and with my brother officers have kept my shoulder to the wheel. This was no more than our duty to a country which supports us, and of which we are justly proud."[12]

The command of the Detroit garrison represented to Brady the culmination of his career, and he came to view the city on the straits as his home, not just a post. He identified with and regarded himself as part of the life of the community. Indeed, the Brady home became a center of entertainment for many civic leaders and numerous other citizens of Detroit. With his sense of loyalty to the area as well as his commitment to his military profession, Brady embodied those qualities that represented the best of the American military tradition. Thus it was not surprising that the valiant veteran of the War of 1812 became the unanimous and enthusiastic choice as the patron for the reorganized militia unit.[13]

Obviously the leaders of the 2 April meeting had thought this subject through with care, for, once the committee had been formally appointed to select a name, its members conferred in a corner and almost immediately reported back to their colleagues that they had chosen the designation "Brady Guards" for their proposed company. The thirty-five assembled volunteers enthusiastically accepted the report and assigned three emissaries "to wait on Maj. Gen. Hugh Brady, U.S.A., and ask permission to use his name for the company."[14]

In seeking Brady's approval of the unit's new appellation, the three representatives informed the veteran officer that such a request had been adopted with unanimous enthusiasm "at a late meeting of numerous young gentlemen in this city, proposing to form themselves into a military corps." They asserted that they wanted their reorganized militia to be named for the general because of his "long and arduous service in the cause of our beloved country" and especially in recognition of the "honorable scars, received in defence of our northwestern frontier, and of Michigan in particular." Had he been so inclined, it would have been difficult for Brady to resist such blandishments. He was not even put off by the importunate request: "As the committee are required to report at 7 this evening, a reply in time for that purpose will be esteemed a favor." Although the sources lack the appropriate detail, it is likely that the representatives of the volunteer company and General Brady had some informal communication prior to the formal re-quest, or else it would have been presumptuous and unacceptably abrupt to have given Detroit's senior soldier so little time to respond. As it was, the old veteran rapidly and graciously replied, "I . . . am happy to . . . express to the 'Brady Guards' . . . my sincere thanks for the compliment they have paid me in adopting my name. . . . Accept gentlemen for the 'Brady Guards' and yourselves individually, the best wishes of your friend and obedient servant." Thus began the long association between Detroit's senior volunteer military group and General Hugh Brady, who identified so enthusiastically with the frontier area he served so well during his career. Brady never forgot that the roots of his and his father's professionalism lay in the militia.[15]

The relationship between the general and the Brady Guards was more than a nominal one. The volunteers were heavily influenced by Brady's advice and character. He was a model of good behavior as well as of martial achievement. Given the strength of Brady's reputation, the prestige of his military standing, and the continued interest he showed in the company, the relationship between the officer and the volunteer unit remained a fruitful one. Not just mutual affection linked Brady and the guards, for the militia played an important role in Detroit when circumstances required the citizen-soldiers to supplement the modest local garrison.

With its new name secured, the reorganized company soon met again to adopt its constitution and bylaws. Indeed, these documents were so frequently revised during the history of the Bradys that redrafting them became almost a hobby of the group. Subsequent alterations, however, tended to involve the reworking of details rather than changes in the original purposes, values, and organizational framework of the guards. A consideration of some of the salient points in the constitution and bylaws serves to illustrate many features of the nature of the unit, without involving one too deeply in the more mundane details.[16]

As a volunteer company, the Bradys comprised a civil and a military institution and made provisions for officials to fill both capacities. The military leaders included a captain, three lieutenants, a quartermaster, and a surgeon, as well as a color sergeant and other noncommissioned officers. The surgeon would not only assume responsibility for treating the illnesses and wounds of the members of the company but would also be in charge of the medical supplies, although the broader control of maintenance and distribution of the property and equipment of the Bradys, to be sure, would be in the hands of the quartermaster. The civil officials who provided the organizational framework to enable the unit to function consisted of a president, a secretary, a treasurer, and an auditor. In addition to these posts there were three "appraisers," who had the responsibility of evaluating the worth of all equipment of the organization and of ensuring proper disposition of any possessions of the group. From the perspective of those interested in the history of the military traditions of the militia, a particularly important and constructive aspect of the assignment given the civil officers in the Bradys devolved from the requirement that "the Secretary shall keep in a book . . . the proceedings of the Guards."[17]

The eligibility criteria prescribed in the original constitution of the Bradys illuminates the composition of the group: "No person under eighteen or over thirty five years of age shall be admitted a member of the Brady Guards." For the regular, nonvoluntary citizen-soldier, the Michigan Militia Act of 1805 stipulated obligatory service for males between the ages of fourteen and fifty. The notion of a middle-aged man adapting himself to the marching pace of boys in their early and mid-teens is startling. By its age criteria, however, the Brady Guards placed itself squarely in the tradition of the volunteer or independent company as contrasted to the regular compulsory militia in American history. The independent units stressed mobility as compared to the more defensive, home-guard posture of the regular militia. The Brady Guards, through the age limits it established for its membership, tried to assure itself of a pool of manpower in which no recruit would be so young that he would lack the maturity of judgment and determination to achieve high standards of military professionalism and, at the same time, in which no individual would be so old that he could not adjust to the demanding rigors of drill and campaigning. The men who reorganized Detroit's volunteer militia into the Brady Guards never intended it to serve simply as a local defense unit. They anticipated that it would achieve a level of professionalism that would enable it to cooperate with the United States Army in maintaining the peace and security of the Old Northwest.[18]

Membership in the Bradys involved exacting requirements. After the original meetings to reorganize the militia in April 1836, any person who wished to join the corps had to make formal application; such a request then had to be endorsed by a member in good standing and supported by the votes of two-thirds of those present and voting at the meeting to which the name was presented. All potential Bradys were required to take its pledge, which set forth the standards of behavior considered appropriate for both a soldier and a gentleman; any member convicted of violating that oath could be expelled by a two-thirds vote.[19]

In line with prevailing military theory of the period, the company exhibited a strong interest in uniforms. Proper dress, it was believed, provided an essential element for achieving a spirit of élan and cohesion in a fighting unit. Particularly among members of volunteer groups in nineteenth-century America, correct attire was a means of developing a sense of professionalism many observers found wanting in the regular militia.[20]

Consequently, the minutes of the Brady Guards reflect a preoccupation with uniforms. Details were continually revised. The early Brady dress included "a dark blue coat, with buff and yellow lace trimmings." Demonstrating the exuberant patriotism of the United States as the nation moved closer to the period of Manifest Destiny, the organization's attire was embellished by buttons decorated with a spread eagle. The elegant Brady regalia also included a leather cap carrying the initials "B.G." in brass and adorned with a plume and "white belts and gloves." The officers of the company in addition wore "gold bullion Epauletts" and "straight swords, with brass scabbards." This, indeed, was an age in which fighting men were expected to dress for the part.[21]

The Brady Guards, as did the unit later when it reorganized as the Detroit Light Guard, also had a band associated with it. The precise relationship of the musical unit to the military organization does not lend itself to easy description, because the nature of the arrangements apparently changed often through the years. The musicians ordinarily did not comprise an integral part of the company, but the militia would nevertheless sponsor or endorse the band. Not only were the musicians commissioned to provide appropriate music for the unit on all suitable occasions, but the bandsmen would also wear distinctive uniforms of "scarlet coats and pantaloons."[22]

To become a full-fledged member of the reorganized company, the recruit had both to sign the Brady Guards pledge and pay the first installment of his dues. Originally twenty-nine individuals met both conditions, and before the end of the month of April at least another twenty-eight had signed. The membership committee optimistically concluded, "There is . . . no doubt of the list swelling to one hundred soon, as the public feel assured of our ultimate success."[23]

The precise number of members of the Brady Guards, which is not always clear from the surviving documents, is less important than the kind of men who chose to commit themselves to this militia organization. In the spring of 1836, joining the Bradys meant assuming an especially heavy financial obligation in addition to the cost of purchasing one's uniform. Originally, every person who signed the pledge would be obligated to pay immediately to the company treasurer five dollars and within thirty days an additional ten dollars. Then, in subsequent periods, further sums to be determined would be required. In the 1830s these were not trifling amounts. Four years after the creation of the Brady Guards, William Henry Harrison, as a presidential candidate, tried to lure voters with the promise, utopian for the time, that if he were elected the workingman would have "two dollars a day and roast beef."[24]

Thus, the financial contribution, as well as the commitment in time and energy, for each member of the company was considerable. Yet the Bradys were not necessarily from affluent backgrounds so much as they were men in the community who had the drive, devotion, and sense of obligation that led them to serve as citizen-soldiers. They created a unit that came to be known as the best in the West and soon acquired a reputation in the New England and Middle Atlantic states. Even among that special elite of the independent militia, Detroit's Brady Guards attained a distinguished name for quality. Moreover, this organization became one of the key volunteer groups that supplemented the more formal institutions of society in holding together the social fabric in Cadillac's old town and the environs of southeastern Michigan. The Brady Guards helped create and maintain the community it would defend.[25]

In their military career, the Bradys aided their namesake in one of the most difficult and unpopular tasks he had to perform during his command at Detroit. The matter involved the enforcement of United States neutrality laws during the Patriot War in Canada in the late 1830s. During the hostilities, Canadian dissidents opposed to British authority often gathered on the American border to attempt to obtain arms for rebels as well as to undertake incursions into Canada. The limited number of federal troops available to General Brady meant that he required the help of the volunteer militia. The Brady Guards was mustered into the United States forces as Captain Rowland's Independent Company, Brady Guards, and served from 5 January until 4 April 1838. The unit also served from 6 December 1838 to 22 February 1839 and from 1 March to 31 May 1839.[26]

The militia gave valuable aid in preventing the violation of American borders either by the Canadian "Patriots" or by British troops. Indeed, during these events, backed by the Brady Guards and a few regular federal military personnel, Hugh Brady responded to an English commander who had threatened to pursue fleeing rebels across the international boundary by ordering his men to "beat back, capture and kill any British who crossed the line." Although the language was somewhat extravagant, the general had made his point and American neutrality was preserved. No royal forces dared to cross the line of flags that Brady had set up on the ice of the frozen Detroit River.[27]

The most serious action involving the Brady Guards was the major military struggle in which the United States engaged between the War of 1812 and the Civil War. This conflict, the Mexican-American War, which lasted from 1846 to 1848, tends to be overlooked by most citizens of this country. The event, when studied in history classes, receives brief mention as a quick and successful campaign launched some twenty years before the War Between the States. The clash with Mexico, however, played a crucial role in the history of America. The episode resulted in Mexico's acquiesence to the United States's annexation of Texas as well as of California and other lands that now comprise the southwestern section of this country. Indeed, the results of this war represented the culmination of the impulse toward Manifest Destiny.[28]

The Mexican-American War also provided American soldiers an opportunity to learn how to adjust their tactics to the improved weapons of the period. Many of the men who would lead the Confederate and Union armies a generation later gained vital experience in the war with Mexico. Consequently, the episode was significant to the future of the Michigan militia and its senior volunteer company, the Brady Guards, even though they did not play as large a role in combat as the soldiers had wished. Although it participated in the Mexican War, the service of the Brady Guards in that struggle was bifurcated; a small part of the unit served as a home guard in the Wolverine State, while most of the other members joined as individuals with the First Michigan Volunteers. The latter regiment did reach Mexico as part of the United States Army and attained experience in the field even though the men arrived in the theater of combat after the principal battles had already occurred.[29]

In the spring of 1847, when United States troops had already begun to win victories on the battlefield, the Detroit militia was torn between pride in the news and regret that the circumstances of the military mobilization had not yet allowed it to enter the fray. "You will warn the Officers Non commissioned Officers & privates of the Brady Guards," wrote Captain Alpheus S. Williams to the company's first sergeant, "to attend a drill at the Armory this evening at 8 oClock. Also a full dress parade tomorrow at 9½ oClock in honor of the Victories in Mexico. You will detail a Squad to see . . . that the gun & caison [sic] are in order."[30]

In October 1847 the First Michigan Volunteers was organized and mustered into federal service. Most members of the Brady Guards flocked to join this unit. Colonel Thomas B. W. Stockton, a West Point graduate, took charge of the regiment, and the Bradys' Alpheus Williams, promoted to lieutenant colonel, assumed the second-in-command position. The many men and officers of the Brady Guards who enlisted in the First Michigan made the Mexican War part of the heritage of Detroit's senior militia organization.[31]

In the meantime a number of the Bradys whose health or family responsibilities did not allow them to campaign in Mexico maintained the company on active duty in Michigan. Under the command of Captain Morgan L. Gage they performed less glamorous but important wartime service by garrisoning such state posts as Fort Mackinac at the Straits and Fort Brady at Sault Sainte Marie. This in turn released regular soldiers for active duty in Mexico.[32]

While their comrades performed constructive yeoman service at home, the Bradys in the First Michigan journeyed to Mexico where they aided their country under difficult and dangerous conditions. Although arriving in the republic to the south after the major fighting had been completed, they nevertheless contributed significantly. For until peace had been formally declared there always existed the threat of guerrilla resistance and possibly counterattacks from a revived Mexican army. The Michiganians helped maintain the safety and effectiveness of the United States Army under trying circumstances, located as they were in an insalubrious setting in a lonely post far from home. Even the able Alpheus Williams plaintively unburdened himself of these feelings in letters to his wife, writing, "Well I am in Mexico—long long away from those I most love." The strain of responsibilities for the colonel and his men was revealed in the following comments when he was organizing his command to escort an expedition: "Spent the whole day in trying to make preparations to March. I know the farther I go away the more constant are my thoughts of you. I shall take good care of myself for your sake & for our little family's sake, but should the occasion offer, of which there is not much chance, while I remember you I shall remind myself that it were better to die honorably than to live to entail upon my children a dishonorable name."[33]

Both bureaucratic details and the dangers involving his unit's responsibilities for convoy duty were on Williams's mind. "You can have no idea of the thousand petty annoyances," the colonel reported, "as well as important preparations that one is obliged to endure on such occasions." He was especially concerned because he knew that the supply train he and his men were to guard contained a considerable amount of gold. Williams understandably felt great stress when he received this assignment, for there was "reliable information that 800 guerrillas with two pieces of artillery were occupying a formidable pass on our route in expectation of this same specie train. Add to this agreeable information the fact that the last two trains up and down the same route have been attacked and in one instance our troops driven in disgrace with considerable loss and you may well suppose that I felt no little responsibility in undertaking my first campaign in Mexico." This Detroit officer, however, met the challenge and completed the mission of escorting the convoy from Vera Cruz to Cordova with efficiency and without mishap.[34]

The unhealthy conditions in Mexico exceeded the danger from enemy irregular troops. "Disease ravaged the ranks worse than grapeshot at fifty yards. Of the regiment's 1,103 men who left the Wolverine State, over 200 died of disease in Mexico." One able officer from the Brady Guards, Isaac S. Rowland, who served as captain of Company E of the First Michigan Volunteers, "although unharmed by ball or blade," suffered permanent health damage and died within two years of the end of the war.[35]

In July 1848 the First Michigan Volunteers returned home from service in Mexico, and the men were mustered out by the end of that month. The Brady Guards, unfortunately, did not regain its former vigor as a voluntary militia organization. A postwar lassitude developed, and there existed less interest in things military in Detroit as well as in many other parts of the country. The account in the records of Friend Palmer, however, that the Brady Guards held no gatherings after June 1847 is simply not correct, although it is difficult to say with precision when the organization stopped meeting. Apparently, the Bradys did not fade away but blended into a successor organization, the Grayson Light Guards, without formally disbanding. At the funeral of General Hugh Brady in April 1851, a number of veterans of the Brady Guards appeared to participate along with members of the Grayson Light Guards and the regular troops from the local garrison. At the end of the ceremony the

Bradys threw their uniform belts into the grave, perhaps marking the symbolic end of the company named in honor of the late general.[36]

The Grayson Light Guards is best thought of as a transitional organization that kept alive the traditions of Detroit's oldest volunteer militia unit until the group was reorganized under the name of the Detroit Light Guard in November 1855. The Graysons provided an opportunity for "young military enthusiasts" in the community to retain their interests in a period of low martial concerns. A great many of the most dedicated Bradys participated in this new unit. The group's name derived from Colonel John B. Grayson, who was stationed with the regular army at Detroit. This officer was not posted in the city for a great length of time, nor did he leave the lasting impression on the community that General Hugh Brady had. The volunteer company, in fact, continued using Grayson's name for only approximately five years. Although the sectional dispute between the North and South centering on the role of slavery in this country began to intensify in the early 1850s, the first half of this decade constituted a relatively peaceful period. Consequently, few services were required from the military, especially in the Michigan area, so the Grayson Light Guards did not have to come to the aid of the community in a martial capacity. But they were "not backward in social matters." Although few sources survive to document the history of the Graysons, those that do typically involve such matters as "thanks . . . to the citizens of Royal Oak, for the reception and salute which welcomed our entrance into their village." Gratitude also was expressed to "the gentlemen of the Fire Department and of Pontiac, for their escort

and kind treatment while we were with them, and for the cordial greeting with which they welcomed us; and to the proprietor of the Hodges House, for the handsome collation so liberally spread before us."[37]

By 1855 national tensions began to intensify as violence erupted between pro- and anti-slavery forces in the Kansas Territory. The newly formed Republican party in the North began to mobilize free-soil sentiment in that region, while in the South the "Fire-eaters," the militant defenders of the South's "Peculiar Institution," rallied for the continuance of bondage for blacks. This tense situation led to a concern for the revitalization of the local volunteer militia.

The impulse culminated in a meeting on 16 November 1855 at which more than forty individuals agreed to create a reformed company under the name Detroit Light Guard. A committee was appointed to secure other members for this organization, and Alpheus S. Williams assumed command of the group.[38] The meeting addressed itself to a perennial problem of volunteer companies— finances—by naming a group "to procure Honorary Members who shall pay $10 per annum." A committee was also selected to work out the details for an appropriate uniform for the company, and an optimistic assumption was made about the future membership of the organization with the provision that "300 copies of the Constitution & By-laws be printed under the direction of the Secretary."[39]

Not only did the Light Guard attempt to raise funds from honorary members, but also from its founding members. Those who were present at the first meeting determined that they would have to make a considerable financial contribution. This included a fourteen-dollar initiation fee, a sum which represented such an investment that the treasurer was able to obtain only ninety dollars from those present at the time. Another seven recruits were able to pay the requisite amount within the next few days. At the second meeting of the organization a copy of the Light Guard pledge was presented to the members for their signatures.[40]

In the next few months the leaders of the reorganized unit efficiently attended to the details of creating an effective company. Each individual who had signed the oath received a copy of the Light Guard Constitution for a fee of twenty-five cents. An armorer was hired to maintain the outfit's weapons, at a salary of seven and a half dollars a month.[41]

Soon the Light Guard was functioning in the best traditions of the volunteer militia. Devotion to drilling and target practice brought it to such a high level of professionalism that in the next generation the Detroit Light Guard would acquire a reputation as one of the best-trained companies west of the Alleghenies and one which compared well with the oldest and most prestigious militia groups of the East. The Detroiters became familiar with the ideas and standards of their colleagues through exchange visits with such key units as the Chicago Light Guard, the Cleveland Grays, and the Milwaukee Light Guard. On one occasion the Detroit company had apparently greeted its guests with such enthusiasm that it had to appropriate money to pay for broken windows "caused by firring [sic] cannon at the reception of the Milwaukee Light Guard June 12th 1859." By early 1857 Detroit's senior military group had received highly flattering reports from Michigan's adjutant general.[42]

Although the Light Guard served primarily as a military organization, it also carried on important social functions in the community. Its annual balls were known for their elegance. The company also sponsored concerts at which its members would turn out in dress uniforms. On such important holidays as Washington's Birthday and the Fourth of July the unit would march in full military regalia, usually accompanied by the Light Guard Band, whose musicians often were paid professionals. Sometimes the parades were followed by appropriate festivities. For example, the Light Guard paid the Russell House, then a fashionable hostelry in downtown Detroit, thirty-five dollars "for refreshments furnished" for 4 July 1857. It had been a grand, if expensive, Independence Day celebration; the militiamen had also spent twenty-two dollars for the services of the musicians.[43]

Sometimes the organization would charter a steamboat to take the company to Fort Wayne for target practice. To make one such excursion more amiable the quartermaster was "instructed to procure a half-barrel of *Ale*, cost not to exceed $4, together with a *tap*." Sometimes the marksmanship of the Light Guardsmen won them shooting contests. Indeed, on one such occasion the membership voted to donate their prize, a barrel of flour, to the Detroit Industrial School, although the school officials requested, and received, five dollars instead as a gift from the Light Guard.[44]

The administration of the company involved a wide variety of technical matters. One such concern led to the approval of a motion "that the Quartermaster procure a sufficient number of Spittoons to accommodate persons who might otherwise deposit Saliva on a *white ash floor* causing thereby stains that nothing short of a hard scrubbing would remove."[45]

The myriad of practical problems and social occasions in which the militia involved itself did not detract from its primary function as a defense force. The ominous developments in national events, which produced a feeling that arms might be needed to preserve the integrity of the country, led the Light Guard to join with other units from the area to sponsor a lecture on military affairs by "Orlando B. Willcox Esq.—late an officer U.S. Army." Soon the speaker and many of those who had listened to him would be putting those principles of war into action on the battlefield. In late 1859 the members of the Light Guard decided to experiment with the structure of their unit and try a battalion organization consisting of two companies.[46]

Although the battalion would be abandoned in favor of the original single company by the time the Civil War had broken out, Detroit's senior militia unit achieved a high degree of professionalism in those last years before the internecine struggle. The Light Guard received "the title of The Banner Company of the Peninsula State" from the inspector general of the Michigan militia. The citizens of Detroit were indeed fortunate, for "no Military Organization in the State [had] expended half the treasure or submitted to greater sacrifices, both of ease and leasure [sic] with a view to impart vigor and character to the System and at the same time to elevate the profession of the Citizen Soldier as the Detroit Light Guard. To say that they reached the Standard erected by the [State Military]Board would be altogether to [sic] tame an expression, but that they *far* exceeded it is certainly within the province of truth."[47]

In the spring of 1859 the Light Guard Battalion at the urging of its commander Alpheus S. Williams took special care "in testing the new Minnie Musket." Soon the militia's life of rigorous training while holding civilian jobs would be replaced by the challenge of serving in the War Between the States, which would determine the nation's future.[48]

Notes

1. Quaife and Glazer, 182.

2. Dunbar, 243–60.

3. *Detroit Gazette*, 27 Sept. 1829. In this history I have chosen to use the form "Brady Guards" rather than "Brady Guard"; although both names appear in the sources, the copy of the first constitution of the organization in the Minutes of the Meeting of 13 Apr. 1836, Brady Guards Papers, R2 Record Book, 1836–1841 and 1876, BHC, uses "Brady Guards," as does the title of the account in vol. 13 of the *Historical Collections: Collections and Researches Made by the Michigan Pioneer and Historical Society.*

4. *Detroit Gazette*, 3 Dec. 1829.

5. Report of Organizational Meeting, 2 Apr. 1836, Brady Guards Papers, R2 Record Book, BHC.

6. Ibid.

7. *Detroit Free Press*, 11 Feb. 1876.

8. Report of Organizational Meeting, 2 Apr. 1836, Brady Guards Papers, R2 Record Book, BHC.

9. *Detroit Saturday Night*, 7 July 1923.

10. Hugh Brady, "General Hugh Brady: A Biographical Sketch of General Hugh Brady, by Himself," *Pioneer Collections: Report of the Pioneer Society of the State of Michigan* 3 (1881): 84.

11. *Detroit Saturday Night*, 7 July 1923; Brady, "General Hugh Brady," 84; George C. Bates, "Reminiscences of the Brady Guards." *Historical Collections: Collections and Researches Made by the Michigan Pioneer and Historical Society* 13 (1888): 542–44.

12. Brady, "General Hugh Brady," 87.

13. *Detroit Saturday Night*, 7 July 1923; Bates, 531–32.

14. Report of Organizational Meeting, 2 Apr. 1836, Brady Guards Papers, R2 Record Book, BHC.

15. Minutes of the Meeting, 6 Apr. 1836, Brady Guards Papers, R2 Record Book, BHC.

16. Minutes of the Meeting, 13 Apr. 1836, Brady Guards Papers, R2 Record Book, BHC.

17. Ibid.

18. Ibid.; Gilpin, *Territory*, 47; Brundage, 16–19.

19. Minutes of the Meeting, 13 Apr. 1836, Brady Guards Papers, R2 Record Book, BHC.

20. Ibid.

21. Ibid.; *Detroit Free Press*, 9 Apr. 1836; Brady Guards, Committee Appointed to Revise the Constitution, Report, 12 Dec. 1836, in Minutes of the Meeting, 2 Mar. 1837, Brady Guards Papers, R2 Record Book, BHC.

22. Minutes of the Meeting, 13 Apr. 1836, Brady Guards Papers, R2 Record Book, BHC.

23. Minutes of the Meeting, 20 Apr. 1836, Brady Guards Papers, R2 Record Book, BHC.

24. Minutes of the Meeting, 13 Apr. 1836, Brady Guards Papers, R2 Record Book, BHC; Quaife and Glazer, 182.

25. Andrew T. McReynolds to P. E. DeMill, 8 Feb. 1876, Montgomery H. Throop to Henry Doty, 10 Apr. 1876, Brady Guards Papers, R2 Record Book, BHC; Andrew Higby to Henry Doty, 10 Apr. 1876, Brady Guards Papers, Reunion Folder, BHC; Bates, 544–45; Frederic S. Isham and Purcell and Hogan, comps., *History of the Detroit Light Guard: Its Records and Achievements* (Detroit, 1896), 14.

26. Bates, 530–46; Hugh Brady, "Reports of General Brady on the Patriot War," *Canadian Historical Review* 31 (Mar. 1950): 56–68. The dates for the federal service of Captain Rowland's Company in 1838 and 1839 are based on United States Department of the Army, *Lineage and Honors,* which has also been accepted by the State of Michigan Military Establishment in General Order no. 54, 27 Aug. 1964. The National Archives staff used slightly different dates of service for technical reasons in their introduction to the microfilm edition of this document, but the variation is not significant.

27. *Detroit Saturday Night*, 7 July 1923; Bates, 536–42.

28. Ernest R. May, *Imperial Democracy: The Emergence of America as a Great Power* (New York, 1961), 7.

29. Walter F. Clowes, *The Detroit Light Guard: A Complete Record of This Organization from Its Foundation to the Present Day* (Detroit, 1900), 20–21.

30. Alpheus S. Williams to First Sergeant Goodnow, 23 Apr. 1847, Brady Guards Papers, 06 Orderly Book, 1836–1876, BHC.

31. Robertson, "Brief Military History" 466; Isham, Purcell, and Hogan, 15; Clowes, 20.

32. Robertson, "Brief Military History" 466; Clowes, 21.

33. Alpheus S. Williams to Jane Larned Williams, 13, 14 Mar. 1848, Alpheus S. Williams Papers, BHC.

34. Alpheus S. Williams to Jane Larned Williams, 14, 20 Mar. 1848, Alpheus S. Williams Papers, BHC; Jeffrey G. Charnley, " 'Neglected Honor,' The Life of General A. S. Williams of Michigan (1810–1878)," (Ph.D. diss., Michigan State University, 1983), 66–67.

35. Charnley, 69; Robert B. Ross, *Early Bench and Bar of Detroit* (Detroit, 1907), 178.

36. Robertson, "Brief Military History" 466; Friend Palmer, Scrapbooks of Miscellaneous Items, 1:103, BHC; Minutes of Special Meeting, 22 Jan. 1848, Brady Guards Papers, R2 Record Book, BHC; *Detroit Free Press*, 18 Apr. 1851.

37. Clowes, 21; Isham, Purcell, and Hogen, 16; Minutes of the Grayson Light Guards, 8 July 1852, Storer.

38. Record of the Company Meeting, 16 Nov. 1855, Detroit Light Guard Minutes, vol. 1, 1855–1860, BHC.

39. Ibid.

40. Record of the Company Meeting, 16, 19 Nov. 1855, Detroit Light Guard Minutes, vol. 1, BHC.

41. Record of the Proceedings of the Board of Direction, 28 Dec. 1855, Detroit Light Guard Minutes, vol. 1, BHC.

42. Isham, Purcell, and Hogan, 19, 39–41; Record of the Proceedings of the Board of Direction, 30 Jan. 1857, 30 Dec. 1859, Detroit Light Guard Minutes, vol. 1, BHC.

43. Record of the Proceedings of the Board of Direction, 22 Sept. 1857, Detroit Light Guard Minutes, vol. 1, BHC; Record of the Company Meeting, 25 Sept. 1857, Detroit Light Guard Minutes, vol. 1, BHC.

44. Record of the Company Meeting, 10 Nov., 29 Dec. 1857, Detroit Light Guard Minutes, vol. 1, BHC; Record of the Proceedings of the Board of Direction, 7 May 1858, Detroit Light Guard Minutes, vol. 1, BHC.

45. Record of the Proceedings of the Board of Direction, 24 Dec. 1858, Detroit Light Guard Minutes, vol. 1, BHC.

46. Record of the Proceedings of the Board of Direction, 19 Nov. 1858, Detroit Light Guard Minutes, vol. 1, BHC; Record of the Company Meeting, 28 Oct. 1859, Detroit Light Guard Minutes, vol. 1, BHC.

47. Clowes, 27; Report of the Inspector General of the Michigan Militia to the State Military Board, 30 May 1859, in Record of the Company Meeting, 31 Oct. 1859, Detroit Light Guard Minutes, vol. 1, BHC.

48. Record of the Company Meeting, 4 Apr. 1859, Detroit Light Guard Minutes, vol. 1, BHC.

Detroit in 1794. Painting discovered by Lady Nancy
Astor and given to the city of Detroit in 1922.
(Courtesy of the Burton Historical Collection,
Detroit Public Library.)

Detroit in 1812. Artist: William Evans. (Courtesy
of the Burton Historical Collection, Detroit Public
Library.)

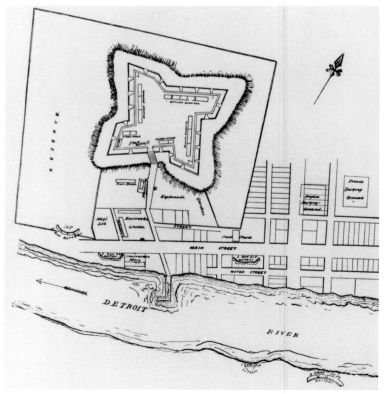

Lewis Cass in 1813, soon after his promotion to brigadier general. Artist: Vanderlyn. Photographic restoration by Frank E. Storer. (Courtesy of the Burton Historical Collection, Detroit Public Library. Original painting in possession of House of Peters, Plandome, New York.)

Colonel Elijah Brush, circa 1813. Artist: Rembrandt Peale. Photographic restoration by Frank E. Storer. (Courtesy of the Detroit Historical Museum.)

Old Arsenal, Detroit, built in 1816 at the corner of Jefferson Avenue and Wayne Street. Weapons the federal government provided to the militia were stored here. Artist: C. W. Sumner. (Courtesy of the Burton Historical Collection, Detroit Public Library.)

Portrait of General Hugh Brady. Date unknown but prior to Brady's promotion from brigadier general to major general in 1848. Artist: Alvah Bradish? Photographic restoration by Frank E. Storer. (Courtesy of Mr. and Mrs. Charles A. DuCharme III, Grosse Pointe Park, Michigan.)

Stevens T. Mason, first elected governor of Michigan. Artist: Elvin Smith. Photographic restoration by Frank E. Storer. (Courtesy of the Detroit Historical Museum.)

Detroit River front in 1819, with Walk-in-the-Water, the first steamship to visit Detroit, in the foreground. Artist: C. W. Sumner. (Courtesy of the Burton Historical Collection, Detroit Public Library.)

The south side of Fort Wayne, near Detroit, after its completion in 1845. Shown are the wooden reinforced ramparts, dry moat, and the demilune used for additional fire power on the river side of the fort. Artist: A. H. Askins. (Courtesy of the Frank E. Storer Collection.)

Pledge of the Brady Guards reaffirmed in 1843. Photographer: Frank E. Storer. (Courtesy of the 225th Infantry Archives.)

General Hugh Brady, circa 1846. Portrait painted and retouched by Frank E. Storer in 1975 from a daguerreotype made by Mathew Brady. (Courtesy of the Detroit Historical Museum.)

Simulated portrait of Isaac S. Rowland, captain of the Brady Guards, drawn by Michael Olbries under the supervision of Frank E. Storer using nineteenth-century descriptions. (Courtesy of the 225th Infantry Archives.)

Major John B. Grayson in 1847. He later became a colonel and died while serving as a brigadier general in the Confederate army. Artist: G. Cooke. Photographic restoration by Frank E. Storer. (Courtesy of the Detroit Commandery # 1, Knights Templar.)

Alpheus S. Williams in the dress uniform of a captain of the Light Guard, circa 1855–60. Artist unknown. Photographic restoration by Frank E. Storer. (Courtesy of the Detroit Historical Museum.)

Sergeant, believed to be David R. Peirce, in the early uniform and bearskin shako of the Detroit Light Guard. Photographer: C. M. Hayes. (Courtesy of the Detroit Historical Museum.)

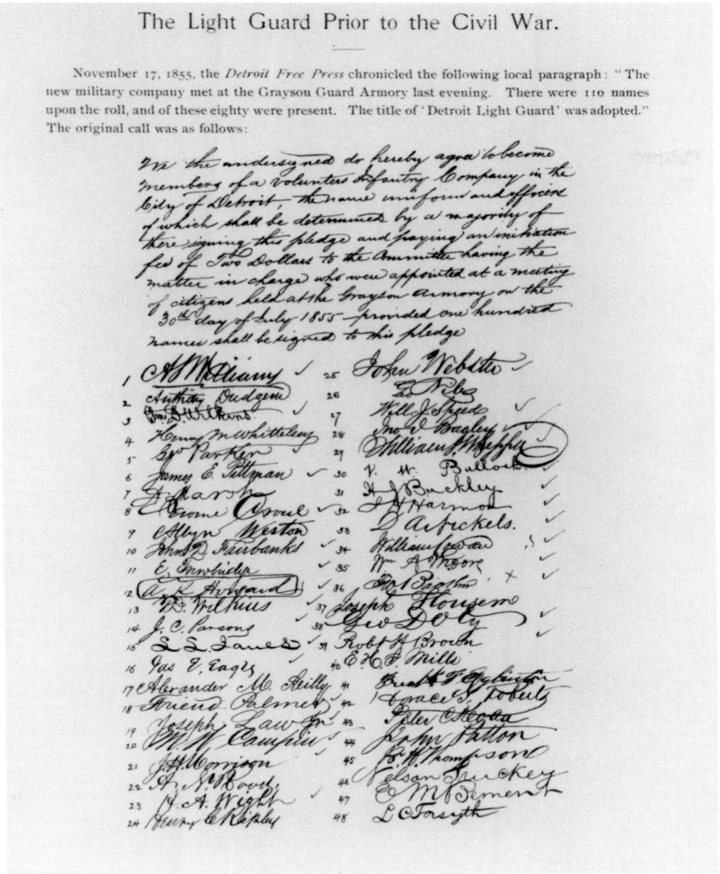

The Light Guard Prior to the Civil War.

November 17, 1855, the *Detroit Free Press* chronicled the following local paragraph: "The new military company met at the Grayson Guard Armory last evening. There were 110 names upon the roll, and of these eighty were present. The title of 'Detroit Light Guard' was adopted." The original call was as follows:

We the undersigned do hereby agree to become members of a Volunteer Infantry Company in the City of Detroit, the name uniform and officers of which shall be determined by a majority of those signing this pledge and paying an initiation fee of Two Dollars to the Committee having the matter in charge who were appointed at a meeting of citizens held at the Grayson Armory on the 30th day of July 1855—provided one hundred names shall be signed to this pledge

1 A. S. Williams
2 Anthony Dudgeon
3 Wm. D. Wilkins
4 Henry M. Whittelsey
5 Geo. Parker
6 James E. Pittman
7 [illegible] Marsh
8 Jerome Croul
9 Allyn Weston
10 John D. Fairbanks
11 E. Trowbridge
12 A. L. Howard
13 [illegible] D. Wilkins
14 J. C. Parsons
15 [illegible]
16 Jas. E. Eagle
17 Alexander M. Reilly
18 Friend Palmer
19 Joseph Lawson
20 W. H. Campau
21 J. H. Morrison
22 A. N. Moore
23 H. A. Wight
24 Henry C. Ripley
25 John Webster
26 [illegible]
27 Will J. Speed
28 Jno. V. Bagley
29 William [illegible]
30 V. W. Bullock
31 H. J. Buckley
32 J. H. Harmon
33 D. Arbickels.
34 William [illegible]
35 Wm. A. Moore
36 [illegible]
37 Joseph [illegible]
38 Geo. Doty
39 Robt. H. Brown
40 E. H. F. Mills
41 [illegible]
42 [illegible]
43 Peter [illegible]
44 John Patton
45 J. H. Thompson
46 Nelson [illegible]
47 E. M. [illegible]
48 L. C. Forsyth

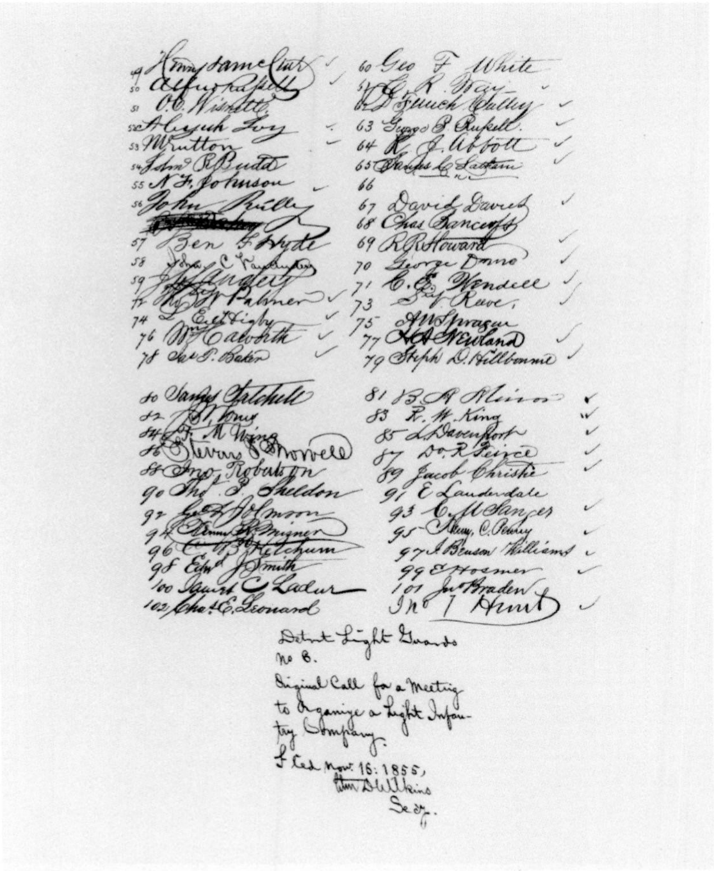

49 [illegible]
50 Alfred Russell
51 O. C. [illegible]
52 [illegible]
53 [illegible]
54 John R. [illegible]
55 N. F. Johnson
56 John [illegible]
57 Ben F. Hyde
58 [illegible] C. [illegible]
59 [illegible]
72 [illegible] Palmer
74 [illegible]
76 Wm. [illegible]
78 [illegible] Baker
60 Geo. F. White
61 [illegible]
62 D. French [illegible]
63 George P. Russell.
64 R. J. Abbott
65 [illegible]
66
67 David Davies
68 Chas. Bancroft
69 R. R. Howard
70 George [illegible]
71 C. E. Wendell
73 [illegible] Reeve
75 A. W. Sprague
77 H. A. Newland
79 Steph. D. [illegible]
80 [illegible]
82 [illegible]
84 [illegible]
86 [illegible]
88 Jno. Robertson
90 Thos. [illegible] Sheldon
92 [illegible]
94 [illegible]
96 [illegible] Ketchum
98 Edwd. J. Smith
100 [illegible] C. [illegible]
102 Chas. E. Leonard
81 [illegible]
83 R. W. King
85 L. Davenport
87 D. R. Peirce
89 Jacob Christie
91 E. Lauderdale
93 C. M. [illegible]
95 Henry C. [illegible]
97 I. Benson Williams
99 E. Hosmer
101 Jno. Braden
Jno. J. Hunt

Detroit Light Guards
No. 6.
Original Call for a Meeting to Organize a Light Infantry Company.
Filed Nov. 16: 1855,
Wm. D. Wilkins
Secy.

Original roll of the Detroit Light Guard, from Isham, Purcell, and Hogan, History of the Detroit Light Guard, *Detroit, 1896, 17–18. (Courtesy of the Frank E. Storer Collection.)*

Detroit Light Guard and Band with the Biddle House and Firemen's Hall in the background, circa 1860. (Courtesy of the Detroit Historical Museum.)

*Roll of the First Michigan Regiment, 17 April 1861, from Isham,
Purcell, and Hogan,* History of the Detroit Light Guard, *Detroit,
1896, 27–28. (Courtesy of the Frank E. Storer Collection.)*

*First Michigan Regiment receiving its colors, 11 May 1861. Photographer: Jex J. Bardwell. (Courtesy of the
Burton Historical Collection, Detroit Public Library.)*

PROCLAMATION!

HEADQUARTERS, ALEXANDRIA, VA., MAY 26, 1861.
Special Orders No. 1.

CAPT. WHITTELSEY, First Michigan Infantry, is detailed for duty as Provost Marshal of this city and such parts of the vicinity as may come within the range of out-posts. He will report for duty immediately to the Commanding Officer until further orders.

Company H is detailed as City Police Guard under command of the Provost Marshal.

The Headquarters of the Police will be the Marshall House. By order of
COL. O. B. WILLCOX.

J. D. FAIRBANKS, Adjutant.

HEADQUARTERS, ALEXANDRIA, MAY 26, 1861.
Orders No. 2.

The undersigned assumes command of the Union Forces in and about Alexandria from the 24th inst.

The peace of the city will be preserved unless attacked by the enemy, when the consequences will rest upon themselves. Private property will be respected and protected by the officers and men of the whole command.

Peaceable citizens will be held inviolate in the persons of themselves, their families and servants.

All disorders will be promptly stopped and offenders arrested and punished.

In ordinary cases the city police will not be interfered with in the performance of their duty, day or night. The Police Guard will form the Military Police of the city, and the Provost Marshal may be applied to by citizens for protection or redress of grievances from soldiers.

Citizens will apply to the Provost Marshal for passes, which he will grant at his discretion, under orders received from the Commanding officer. By order of
COL. O. B. WILLCOX.

J. D. FAIRBANKS, Adjutant.

GALLOWAY & O'DONNELL, PRINTERS, FIRST REG. MICH. VOL.

Special orders for Alexandria, Virginia, 26 May 1861. Photographer: Frank E. Storer. (Courtesy of William Rasmussen, Royal Oak, Michigan.)

Charles M. Lum as colonel of the Tenth Michigan Infantry, August 1863. Artist: John Mix Stanley. (Courtesy of the Detroit Historical Museum.)

Orlando B. Willcox, former colonel of the First Michigan Regiment, after he had been promoted to brigadier general. (Courtesy of the Burton Historical Collection, Detroit Public Library.)

First Michigan Regiment ready for inspection at Fort Wayne, circa May 1861. Photographer: Jex J. Bardwell. (Courtesy of the Burton Historical Collection, Detroit Public Library.)

Civil War

The history of the Light Guard is inextricably bound with the history of the United States. No episode of this story involved more dramatic and challenging events than the War Between the States, a key event in the story of the American republic. The Civil War, 1861–65, determined the nature of the federal Union and its future as an effective national government. The struggle also ended the practice of slavery, which oppressed most black Americans living in the fifteen states that still supported this institution in 1861. When eleven of the slave states attempted to secede from the Union after the victory of Lincoln and the Republicans in the 1860 election, a war to preserve the Union resulted. Although the president-elect and his party opposed the extension of slavery into any of the western territories that had not yet become states, they promised not to interfere with the so-called "Peculiar Institution" where it already existed.

Southern leaders, however, became convinced that the tide of opinion had so turned against them in the federal Union that they would not be treated fairly. As a result, most of the slave states, led by South Carolina in December 1860, tried to leave the Union that winter to form the new Confederate States of America in February 1861. The other ten states involved were Mississippi, Florida, Alabama, Georgia, Louisiana, Texas, Virginia, Arkansas, Tennessee, and North Carolina. The mountain counties of western Virginia chose, however, to stay with the United States and in 1862 were admitted to the Union as the separate state of West Virginia. The border slave states of Missouri, Kentucky, Maryland, and Delaware also refused to attempt to secede, although large minorities within their boundaries supported the Confederacy. Terms such as Union, federal, and North are designations for those who during the war upheld the cause of preserving the unity of the United States. Confederate, rebel, South, and secessionist can be considered equivalent terms in describing their opponents. Also in viewing the years from 1861 to 1865, it should be kept in mind that President Lincoln originally regarded the objective of the war to be simply the restoration of the Union. As the cost in human lives and suffering grew during the protracted struggle, the chief executive, as well as the Northern public, became convinced that slavery was the ultimate cause of the conflict and had to be eliminated if the Union were to be permanently restored.

In Detroit and Michigan citizens followed these events with apprehension. On 8 January Detroit citizens fired a one-hundred-gun salute on Campus Martius, both to commemorate one of the heroic moments in America's short history, the victory of Andrew Jackson over the British at the Battle of New Orleans in the War of 1812, and to pay tribute to Major Robert J. Anderson. This officer commanded the beleaguered federal garrison that still maintained control of Fort Sumter, which dominated the harbor of Charleston, South Carolina, one of the leading seaports of the Confederacy. Indeed, one of the popular tunes in Detroit at that time was "Major Anderson's Quick-Step." The Masonic Grand Lodge of Michigan adopted a unanimous resolution in support of actions to hold the United States together. The outgoing governor of Michigan, Moses Wisner, urgently declared in his farewell speech that "the Union . . . must and shall be preserved." The next day the man who would be the wartime governor of Michigan, Austin Blair, having taken the oath of office, pledged "the

whole military power of the State" to aid the federal government.[1]

With the inevitability of a Greek drama, national events moved toward a tragic outcome. On 12 April Confederate artillery batteries in Charleston harbor opened fire on Fort Sumter, and on the following day Major Anderson surrendered. He and his men were permitted to depart in United States naval vessels. A wave of outrage swept through the North. After this firing on Fort Sumter there would be no turning back from four bloody years of civil war. Detroit and its Light Guard were going to do their share in the ensuing struggle, and theirs would be a costly contribution.[2]

Two days after the attack, Lincoln sent out a call to the states for seventy-five thousand militia troops to serve for a period of ninety days to suppress the rebellion. Governor Blair in response issued a proclamation asking for one regiment of Wolverine State volunteers to fill the president's quota. Detroiters, joining their brethren throughout the Union in rallying around the flag in those troubled days of April, raised the Stars and Stripes everywhere in the town, on buildings, homes, and public conveyances. The city on the straits became a virtual sea of United States flags. The outpouring of public-spirited sentiment and the picturesque, patriotic displays, however, did not hide the widespread anxiety about the future of the nation.[3]

The Detroit Light Guard led the way in volunteering for the new ninety-day regiment, just as its members had always been among the first to respond to crisis. On the evening of 17 April the Light Guard met at its armory and enthusiastically and unanimously offered the services of the company to the state and the nation. Admiring spectators added to the spirit of the occasion with loud shouts of approval.[4]

James E. Pittman, the captain of the Light Guard, unable for personal reasons to enter federal service, resigned and recommended the unit's vigorous First Sergeant Charles M. Lum to succeed him. The membership accepted the suggestion without dissent. The next morning the rolls of the company were opened for members who had not yet had the opportunity to sign up officially for Civil War service. Other recruits were then allowed to enlist until the company achieved its maximum strength. So many volunteers rushed forward to join the unit that many had to be turned away, much to their dismay. As the Light Guard quickly prepared to leave for war, the patriotic fervor increased in Detroit. A dramatic moment occurred when the company "participated in the ceremony of raising the American flag from the roof of the postoffice. . . . In the center window of the building, on the second story, was a transparency: 'The Union—one and perpetual; what God has joined together let no man put asunder.'"[5]

One of the most notable aspects of the actions of the Light Guard and the others who answered Lincoln's call for volunteers was their willingness to risk their lives for an abstraction, an ideal. As a prominent Detroiter, T. W. Palmer, observed, "The men who fell at Manassas were not mercenary soldiers. They did not enlist for the eleven dollars a month and board. They were animated by the loftiest patriotism. . . . The Spartans fought to prevent invasion and consequent subjugation. Our men fought not for any such purpose,

but for the triumph of constitutional liberty. Their homes and all their selfish interests were safe. They fought the battle for humanity, for the world, for posterity."[6]

The first of May had been selected as the official date of muster for the First Michigan Regiment. The Light Guard, as the state's oldest militia unit, became Company A of the new regiment. Colonel Orlando B. Willcox accepted command of the First Michigan. His qualifications for this task included training at West Point and service in the regular army for a number of years. He had resigned from the service and had settled in Detroit to pursue a career as a lawyer but had continued his military interest in civilian life by joining the Light Guard. His combination of regular army professionalism and association with Detroit's volunteer militia made him a natural choice to lead Michigan's ninety-day regiment. This group, Michigan's earliest contribution to the defense of the Union, consisted of 798 officers and men.[7]

Recruits for the new regiment converged on Detroit from various parts of the state, and Fort Wayne became the center of feverish military activity. As the Light Guard, now Company A, and its comrades of the First Michigan prepared for war, the citizens of Detroit overwhelmingly rallied to the support of the federal government. A special concert was held to raise funds for the families of Michigan soldiers, and the distinguished local clergyman D. Bethune Duffield wrote for the occasion a special patriotic poem that was set to music.[8]

In keeping with the serious and dangerous nature of the mission of the First Michigan, solemn religious services were held at Fort Wayne. Red, white, and blue banners waved everywhere throughout Detroit, and groups of townspeople alternated between praying for the Union and for the safety of their fellow Detroiters going off to war. Patriotic songs marked enthusiastic public gatherings as the time approached for the soldiers' departure. Those members of the unit who for reasons of health or age or family responsibility were not able to join Company A formed the Detroit Light Guard Reserve Corps to provide local protection during the war. Meanwhile, at Fort Wayne disciplined training continued. The drilling involved an intensive schedule, usually nine hours a day. If city troops, because of the sedentary nature of many of their occupations, tended not to be quite so physically fit as some of their country cousins at the start of the war, the intensive preparation that the Light Guardsmen underwent in the spring of 1861 soon toughened them to face the best trained of their opponents in gray.[9]

The rigorous, demanding drilling soon resulted in the widespread affliction of "blistered feet and sore joints." Such momentary inconveniences, however, did not diminish the enthusiasm of the Light Guardsmen preparing for the battle to save the Union. Many individuals were so eager to join the unit that, once the ranks of the company were filled, a number of would-be recruits offered generous financial inducements to anyone willing to give up his place in the company, but no one in Company A agreed to do so. Indeed, so anxious were the Light Guardsmen to enter federal service that, when the men received their official examinations by an army surgeon, without exception each of them stated "that he 'never felt better in his life.'"[10]

By the end of the first week of May, preparations for the departure of the First Michigan were virtually complete. In its last few days at Fort Wayne, training, especially target practice, intensified. In Lansing the governor and the legislature continued to enact the measures necessary to facilitate Michigan's war effort. At the same time Dorothea Dix, a pioneer in professional nursing, appealed from Washington to Michigan women to serve in military hospitals.[11]

By 12 May Colonel Willcox had issued the final orders regarding the First Michigan, and the women of Detroit had presented the regiment with a banner and cockades in a moving ceremony on Campus Martius. Since the troops were not leaving until the early evening of 13 May, that day witnessed much activity. The boats providing transportation between the city and Fort Wayne were filled to capacity with friends and relatives, as well as the curious who wanted to be part of the excitement. In such an atmosphere any attempt to have the usual daily drill would have been impossible, and indeed the men of the First Michigan had already had more than ample practice. "It was estimated that more than 10,000 persons visited the Fort during the day." As townspeople returned from Fort Wayne, the ferries headed in the opposite direction were loaded to capacity with officers and men who had been able to make one last trip home to say their farewells to family and friends.[12]

The ferry belonging to the Detroit and Milwaukee Railroad conveyed the members of the First Michigan from Fort Wayne to the docking area on the river where the vessels *Illinois* and *May Queen* were waiting to take the regiment to Cleveland. The First Michigan with its Company A, then, left

Detroit amid the excited cheers of massed citizens, a blaze of fireworks, and band music ranging from the martial air of "Hail, Columbia" to the sentimental strains of "The Girl I Left Behind Me." The military flotilla arrived at Cleveland early the next morning. As the transports approached the docks of the city, a special signal of the ships' horns alerted the regiment's officers to prepare their men to disembark as rapidly and efficiently as possible. Once ashore the Michiganians marched to breakfast in strict military order and afterwards entrained for the next segment of their journey. Company A occupied the first car of the train and served as the advance guard, providing protection for the headquarters unit, which rode in the second car.[13]

The journey of the troops through Ohio and into Pennsylvania took on aspects of a triumphal procession. Clevelanders had applauded the Michiganians with all the enthusiasm that might have been reserved for a favorite Buckeye unit. As the twenty-one-car train moved through the Ohio countryside, the local people hailed it as if it contained a Roman legion returning from a major victory. At various stops young women distributed cakes and pies among the Wolverine soldiers; sometimes locks of hair and on at least one occasion a card on which was inscribed, "God bless you," were presented to the men of the First Michigan. At this time of great anxiety about the future of the Union, citizens were reassured by the trainload of troops representing the best of Michigan's militia units.[14]

Changing trains in Pittsburgh, the regiment continued on the Pennsylvania Railroad over a particularly rough roadbed. As the First Michigan hurried toward Washington, proud De-

troiters eagerly consumed every scrap of news that correspondents could provide about their state's contingent. The lack of facilities forced Company A to ride in the baggage car, but the Light Guardsmen demonstrated themselves equal to the minor indignity of the occasion. A democracy of discomfort governed the trip as officers and men shared floors and car platforms with each other, suitcases, and equipment. The distress of meals missed in the course of difficult travel with minimal facilities and rude accommodations must have been at least in part compensated for by such sights as an aging farmer who, as the troops rode past him, "dropped his hoe, threw off his hat, and, raising his clasped hands, seemed to invoke the blessing of heaven upon the passing train."[15]

At Altoona the First Michigan received some tangible physical encouragement from a hot breakfast provided by local citizens. At Harrisburg the troops had an opportunity to detrain and restore their vigor by marching to nearby Camp Curtin. Here they joined militiamen from the Keystone State and were "issued fresh beef, bread and coffee." Many of the Michiganians, however, had a problem because they had no "mess gear" and a good many of them lacked cooking experience. There were exceptions, such as one not overly modest soldier, who recalled, "I doubt if there was a man in A company, except your humble servant, who had ever cooked a thing in his life, and my example of broiling a strip of beef on the end of a rammer and making coffee in my tin cup was soon followed by the other amateur chefs."[16]

After an active day at Camp Curtin in which the First Michigan, including the Light Guard Band, had impressed the Pennsylvania military and civilians with its skill and professionalism on parade, the men of the regiment were ready to relax with a night on the town. They were upset to learn that Colonel Willcox had issued orders confining them to camp for the night. Adding to the distress over their confinement was the revelation that the officers of the First Michigan had been invited to a reception at the executive mansion by Pennsylvania's Governor Curtin. So some of the intrepid members of Company A, feeling that the strict discipline imposed on them was excessive for one of their last nights before reaching the area of combat, decided to break their orders. Consequently, by tactics they never revealed, about twenty of the Light Guardsmen managed to leave camp that night, despite commands to sentinels that no passes be honored at the gates. A bemused Colonel Willcox reacted more with wry humor and surprise than anger when, during a conversation at a café with some of his Pennsylvania brother officers to whom he had proudly been describing the discipline of his regiment in general and Company A in particular, he spied a number of the errant Light Guardsmen.[17]

The next morning the men of the First Michigan left Harrisburg to continue their journey to Baltimore, where they would change trains for Washington by marching from one railroad station to another. Upon reaching Baltimore, they found themselves in a tense and potentially dangerous situation. Maryland was one of the border states, a slave state that had chosen to remain within the Union but whose people were deeply divided in their loyalties to the Northern and Southern causes. In the confused days of May 1861 federal authorities simply were not certain how much secessionist sentiment existed in the Baltimore area.

Just prior to the arrival of the First Michigan, a unit of New England troops attempting to pass through the town had suffered harassment from local Confederate sympathizers.[18]

As a result, local officials advised Colonel Willcox to skirt Baltimore for the safety of his Michigan militia. The commander, however, would have nothing to do with such timid tactics. Firmly he averred that "he would either go through the city or over it." He insisted on marching the First Michigan on the most direct route to the other station. In this bold maneuver Willcox had Company A serve as an advance guard of the regiment. Willcox ordered his troops to load their weapons, and then proudly they paraded through the streets of Baltimore with their band playing "The Star-Spangled Banner," lest any local ears had already become unused to hearing the national anthem. The First Michigan marched with enthusiasm through streets lined with spectators. The Wolverines made a tremendously positive impression on the people of the town, and the Light Guard Band received particular praise from local commentators who described the Michiganians as "the finest in appearance of any who have yet reached this city."[19]

Colonel Willcox's daring tactics worked. Without hindrance and with the applause of the citizens, the First Michigan reached the proper depot and entrained for Washington. The soldiers did not arrive in the capital until nearly ten o'clock in the evening, tired, bedraggled, but hardly unnoticed. Indeed, from their first moments there, the First Michigan seemed to capture the imaginations of the Washingtonians and the capital's press corps. "'The Michigan Rifle Regt. came into town last night about 10 o'clock, marching from the depot up the Avenue to Eleventh Street,' the Washington correspondent of the *New York Evening Post* informed his newspaper. 'They were preceded by a splendid band of music which soon aroused our citizens, and long before they had reached the quarters assigned to them, hundreds of people were out to give them welcome. The enthusiasm of the crowd was irrepressible, for this was the first Western regiment that had arrived at the capital.'"[20]

To Americans of 1861, to whom the Pacific Coast seemed to be at the other end of the world, Michigan did indeed represent the West. The First Michigan had reached the capital at a particularly tense time. The rebels pressed closely upon the boundaries of the District of Columbia, and Southern "troops flaunted their flag on Arlington Heights, . . . rebel pickets patroled [sic] the banks of the Potomac and bivouacked under the old trees that shade the grave of Washington." Any reinforcements were welcome, but particularly those who were the first arrivals from the Northwest, perhaps the most strongly nationalistic section of the Union at that time. This situation provided the background for the famous remark attributed to Abraham Lincoln, "Thank God for Michigan."[21]

The citizens of Washington enthusiastically welcomed the First Michigan as badly needed reinforcements who heralded more aid from a distant and dynamic section of the country. Soon the Wolverine officers and band called at the White House. Lincoln, delighted with the arrival of the crack Michigan regiment and charmed by the concert of Major Elderkin and the justly renowned Light Guard Band, appeared at a second-floor window to acknowledge the concert. The

Light Guardsmen vigorously applauded him, and the chief executive responded to this enthusiasm by inviting the Michiganians into the East Room of the White House, where the company officers were presented to him. Lincoln had so enjoyed the Light Guard Band that he also asked to meet the musicians. They made such a favorable impression that the band was chosen for the signal honor of alternating with the Marine Band and a Rhode Island regimental band in giving concerts three times a week on the grounds behind the White House.[22]

Soon, however, the First Michigan would be called upon for services more military than musical. In that particularly confused period in the early days of the war, the federal government especially concerned itself with establishing defenses for the capital against nearby rebel forces. A substantial body of Union troops from the East had gathered in the District of Columbia by the time the Michiganians arrived there. Confederate soldiers were "encamping and drilling almost within sight of Washington." Across the Potomac River, the town of Alexandria, controlled by rebels, constituted a dagger pointed at the jugular vein of the capital. Lincoln considered it imperative to reestablish United States authority in that Virginia town. Early in the morning hours of 23 May, the day after Virginia formally made its decision to enter the Confederacy, "in bright moonlight . . . Federal troops moved quietly across the Washington bridges to fortify the hills and ridges commanding the ten-mile-square area of the capital."[23]

The forces that advanced on Alexandria included troops from Michigan and New York. Of these Northerners, the men of Company A led the way, so the Light Guardsmen in that campaign became the first federal soldiers to set foot on soil held by the Confederate army. In carrying out this assignment the Light Guard troops found themselves allied with the New York Fire Zouaves organized from the ranks of the New York Fire Department by Elmer E. Ellsworth. This officer had once read law in Abraham Lincoln's office and then practiced in Chicago. Ellsworth had been active in the Chicago Zouaves, and his militia company and the Detroit Light Guard had exchanged visits. Having moved to New York, he organized a new militia company and found himself once again associated with the Light Guard in the Alexandria campaign.[24]

Hidden by the dark cover of the early morning hours, the First Michigan arrived at the bridge connecting Washington with Alexandria. Under the leadership of Orlando Willcox, the regiment crossed rapidly the "Long Bridge, driving in the rebel pickets" before it. Company A, once across the river, quickly moved into the town, and at about the same time Ellsworth and the New York Fire Zouaves reached it by ship. The Union troops entered Alexandria at different points and converged on the town square according to carefully arranged plans. "The whole enterprise had been planned with careful secrecy and was executed with precision." No significant opposition from the startled rebels hindered the federal forces, which overwhelmed the unprepared Southern defenders.[25]

The mayor of Alexandria, awakened at an inconveniently early hour by the Northern troops, at once surrendered the city. A defiant rebel raised the Stars and Bars, the flag of the Confederacy, above his inn, the Marshall House. Colonel Ellsworth, "accompanied by an aide, the regimental chaplain, a New York Tribune correspondent, and a squad of soldiers," entered the hostelry. The Zouave commander intended personally to pull down the offending Southern banner. Ellsworth started up the stairs to the roof accompanied by the clergyman and the journalist. A bodyguard would have been more in order for the colonel, for the proprietor, a "violent secessionist," waited at the bottom of the attic staircase for Ellsworth after he had pulled down the Confederate flag. In an uncontrolled fury the rebel shot and killed the colonel. Moments later one of Ellsworth's Zouaves fatally wounded the assassin.[26]

The capture of Alexandria required the victorious troops to consolidate their position. Located on the border between Union and Confederate territory, the federal forces found themselves in a precarious situation. Precautions had to be taken against guerrilla attacks by irregular Southern forces or large-scale counterattacks from the main Confederate army. The First Michigan and the Zouaves bivouacked in an area as historic and beautiful as it was strategic. Shuter's Hill dominated the valley behind Alexandria and commanded all of the land approaches to the city except from the north. The hill's striking vista included Washington. The Light Guardsmen from their camp could see two important symbols of national authority, the Capitol and the White House. No wonder that George Washington had not only quartered his army at Shuter's Hill during the War for Independence but had also later considered it as a location for the capital of the United States.[27]

The First Michigan men drilled regularly to keep up their military skills as well as their physical fitness. At the same time the Wolverines and their New York comrades in arms worked rapidly to fortify the area to repel any Confederate attack. When Shuter's Hill had been converted into a formidable redoubt, the troops named it Fort Ellsworth after the late colonel. The immediate threat to the members of the Union forces stationed there involved the hit-and-run tactics of the rebels in the area. These Southern raiders would often strike quickly at Northern guards stationed on the perimeter of their camp; at other times they would attempt to pick off scattered groups of two or three Union soldiers if they could find them in an isolated spot in the woods or on a lonely road. Such rebel troops were colloquially, although not affectionately, known as "bushwhackers." These guerrillas were a constant problem for the First Michigan even though the enemy failed in its attempts to harm the regiment.[28]

The Michiganians and other troops stationed at Fort Ellsworth spent considerable time scouting the surrounding area to gather intelligence about the Confederate army in northern Virginia. In assembling information, the Wolverines also engaged in the time-honored, if not officially sanctioned, practice of foraging. Soldiers roamed the countryside to appropriate food and other necessities for themselves and their comrades. This acquisition of supplies may not always have been legal, but it has deep roots in the history of warfare. Foraging in the spring of 1861 did produce a generous supply of pork and poultry with which the Michiganians and their allies supplemented their standard army rations.[29]

Thus the members of Company A and the others of the First Michigan lived briefly after the Alexandria campaign an existence characterized by the tedium of drill, marred occasionally by the threat of death from enemy raids, but interspersed with moments of light-hearted country life. Indeed, on Independence Day 1861, the chief challenge to the Light Guardsmen was how to divide ten dollars in regimental funds that their commander, Captain Charles Lum, announced would be available for a celebration. The company was split into factions of those who wanted to express their patriotism by drinking and those by smoking. Finally, in the best American tradition, a compromise was reached: they purchased a keg of liquid refreshments and spent the balance of the money on plug tobacco.[30]

The men of Company A were eager to engage in more serious fighting, and this impatience accorded with the mood of the majority of the Northern public. Beginning with the move into Alexandria, the authority of the United States had been reestablished in a number of key areas around Washington. The ease with which this had been done caused a number of Northern leaders to underestimate the professionalism of the Confederate army. Soon supporters of the Union were demanding action, and large cities and small towns in the North echoed with cries of "On to Richmond!" This sentiment for rapid and decisive military action, "like an immense tidal wave, . . . reached and flooded the executive and war departments, and poor old Gen. Scott felt himself forced to order an onward movement against his own good judgment." Winfield Scott, the seventy-four-year-old general in chief of the United States Army, had doubts in the early summer of 1861 about the readiness of the Union army for a major effort but simply could not resist the well-intentioned but misinformed optimism among Northerners, including

President Lincoln. The chief executive decided that the federal army must move at once against the rebels. The resulting defeat, the First Battle of Bull Run, would lead the anguished General Scott to lament to the President, "Sir, . . . I am the greatest coward in America. . . . I did not stand up, when my army was not in condition for fighting."[31]

The events preceding the battle that became a disaster for the Northern army began placidly enough for the men of the Light Guard. They had been deployed from Fort Ellsworth to a nearby spot called Cloud's Mill. They remained in that camp until mid-July. In the meantime, the First Michigan's colonel, Orlando B. Willcox, had become the acting commander of the Second Brigade, which included the Fire Zouaves, the Thirty-eighth New York Regiment, and an artillery unit called Arnold's Battery. This brigade in turn served in a division commanded by General Heintzelman.[32]

During the Civil War the South followed a largely defensive strategy. If the United States government simply allowed the Confederacy to exist, it would entail a kind of de facto recognition of an independent nation. To maintain the integrity of the United States, the federal government had to go on the offensive as soon as possible. The actions of the rebel government meant that the First Michigan was stationed in an area that was a key region in the war as early as the summer of 1861, for "on May 21 the Confederate Congress accepted Virginia's invitation to move the capital from overcrowded, wilting Montgomery to the bustling industrial and commercial center of Richmond."[33]

One of the most politically influential New York dailies well summarized pro-Union sentiment when it "put the slogan 'Forward to Richmond' on its masthead and kept it there day after day, thundering editorially that the Rebel Congress must not be allowed to meet on July 20." Northern opinion increasingly demanded that the federal armies engage the Confederates in battle. The main Union force in the Washington area consisted of thirty-five thousand troops assembled by General Irvin McDowell; this army included the First Michigan. Camped across the Potomac from the capital, this body would of course be the key unit in any move toward Richmond. "Twenty-five miles away a Confederate force of 20,000 under General Beauregard deployed on the south bank of Bull Run covering the key rail junction at Manassas." Lincoln instructed McDowell to draw up forthwith plans to attack Beauregard's army and if these were approved to execute them at once. McDowell pleaded with the president for more time to prepare his troops for battle. The chief executive refused what he regarded as his commander's attempt at procrastination. Lincoln's judgment no doubt was affected by the political pressures stemming from the insistent public demand that the federal government take some immediate, strong action to suppress the rebellion. When McDowell argued that his soldiers were not yet ready for a campaign, the chief executive replied, "You are green, it is true, . . . but they are green also; you are all green alike." Then the president told his field commander in clear language to begin his campaign. The unfortunate general obeyed his commander in chief, leading his men into action—and into disaster.[34]

Contributing to an already complicated and perilous situation for McDowell was the fact that in addition to Beauregard's twenty thousand men, there also existed fifty miles away a force of twelve thousand rebels commanded by one of the ablest officers in the Confederacy, General Joseph E. Johnston. If the two Southern armies combined, it would create an awesome opposition for the Union troops. As the Northern soldiers advanced, Willcox's brigade, including the First Michigan, moved toward Fairfax Courthouse, where a heavy concentration of the enemy had come together. The Wolverines played a key role in driving the Confederates out of the Fairfax area. Their achievement became part of a growing air of success and enthusiasm that characterized the Union troops moving more deeply into northern Virginia in mid-July. McDowell's army seemed poised on the brink of a great victory, even though the group lacked a high degree of professionalism and extensive experience. "It was a heterogeneous array—Zouaves in red fezzes and baggy Turkish trousers, Garibaldi guards in long-plumed hats, Wisconsin boys in homespun gray, Massachusetts boys in blue, a Minnesota regiment in black felt hats, black pants, and red-checkered lumberjack shirts, with a small detachment of regulars."[35]

The Northerners, however, headed for disaster. Their opponents "had learned of McDowell's plans from Rose O'Neal Greenhow, head of a confederate spy ring in Washington." With the aid of this information the astute General Johnston outmaneuvered the Union forces in the Shenandoah Valley and then swiftly transported his men by rail to join those at Manassas Junction on the eve of the clash. The ensuing engagement, the First Battle of Bull Run, also called Manassas, pitted McDowell's relatively inexperienced attacking group against a Confederate army of comparable strength. Tough and resourceful soldiers, the rebel troops, somewhat less green than their Union counterparts, despite President Lincoln's pronouncement, had the further advantages of fighting on their home terrain and of having the particularly imaginative and flexible leadership of their officers.[36]

The encounter of McDowell's and Beauregard's armies took place on 21 July. The leaders of the federal government expected a decisive victory over the Southern forces. "Carriages from Washington filled with congressmen and assorted spectators drove out to 'see the Rebels get whipped.'" At first, as the two armies clashed along the banks of the Bull Run, the situation seemed propitious for the Northerners. Whatever their lack of experience, they fought bravely and effectively. Soon, however, the veteran Confederates turned the tide of battle in their favor. Well into the afternoon, both President Lincoln and General Scott received reports that the struggle at Manassas had been won by the Northern forces. Then the news began to change; distraught cabinet members rushed to the White House with information that the conflict had taken a disastrous turn. By the time the startled president reached the War Department, a telegram had arrived with the shocking message: "General McDowell's army in full retreat through Centerville. The day is lost. Save Washington and the remnants of this army. . . . The routed troops will not reform."[37]

What part had the First Michigan and the Light Guardsmen of Company A played in this battle? Two days before the struggle, the First Michigan and the rest of Willcox's Second Brigade had rendezvoused at Centerville and bivouacked in the midst of a driving rain. The downpour, according to a member of Company A, "lasted nearly all night, and drenched us to the skin as we lay in the furrows of a fallow field, without even the shelter of a pup tent. Sunrise next morning disclosed us standing around the fires, stripped of our clothing, which hung to dry on the butts of our muskets, held upright by driving the bayonets into the ground. The more modest of us clothed ourselves in a cloud of tobacco smoke." On the day before the battle the Michiganians were able to dry out and obtain some rest. The First Michigan entered the fray early in the afternoon of the twenty-first. After the preparations of the brigade had been completed to Colonel Willcox's satisfaction, the unit began moving forward at 6:00 A.M., reaching its destination about noon. At that point the Second Brigade had already put in an exhausting day involving rapid movements "over roads thick with dust." During their travel, moreover, the men had available to them only "a scant supply of water."[38]

The men of the First Michigan enjoyed a brief respite and then had to push on again. The Wolverine soldiers were soon caught up in the complex maneuvers of McDowell's army. Arnold's Battery took a position on the high ground just beyond the Bull Run, and the First Michigan assumed the task of protecting this unit. Colonel Willcox led the Fire Zouaves and the New York Thirty-eighth forward to attack the Confederates. In the fighting that ensued, Willcox's men were soon outmaneuvered by Southern forces, which included some Virginians led by a former professor of military tactics at the Virginia Military Institute who became famous under the nickname of Stonewall Jackson. As the situation became desperate the First Michigan rushed to aid the embattled Fire Zouaves. "Moving in column by platoon along the slope of the hill under the fire of the enemy's batteries we lost one color-bearer and several of our men." The First Michiganians hurled themselves against the rebels. Fierce and confused fighting followed. The very speed of the Wolverines' advance left them in doubt about the location of their foe. Chaos ensued and at one point failure to understand clearly an order caused part of the line to fall back. Quickly, however, the Michigan soldiers reformed their ranks. "Led by Colonel Willcox, . . . the regiment, responding to the wave of his cap with a cheer, . . . charged down the slope on the enemy's battery."[39]

For a time the First Michigan, under the most difficult of circumstances, pressed forward and advanced deeply into rebel-held territory. But the gunfire of the Wolverines enabled Confederate commanders to locate the positions of the Michiganians. Thus, the enemy, aided by fresh troops from Johnston's army under the able command of General Kirby-Smith, effectively executed a flanking movement, outmaneuvering the First Michigan. Soon the regiment found itself raked by continuous rifle and artillery fire. The Wolverines, inexperienced as they were in battlefield action, held up surprisingly well. They maintained their ranks and discipline in a situation that might have broken the spirit of battle-hardened troops. The men of Company A fought as intrepidly as any of their fellows of the First Michigan and carried on the professionalism and esprit de corps of the Light Guard. The Michiganians hoped for reinforcements that did not come. In the meantime the enemy kept up its devastating fire and at the same time advanced with large numbers of infantry upon the beleaguered Wolverines. By late afternoon the Second Brigade was overwhelmed by the attacking rebels. Orlando Willcox had his horse shot from under him and was himself wounded and taken prisoner.[40]

Captain Charles Lum, who had been serving as acting commander of Company A, suffered dramatically in the battle but managed to avoid capture. After having been severely wounded in a series of incredible adventures, he took over the driving of the horses of the ambulance in which he was being carried, and later rode horseback in his escape. Despite his weakened state, Lum made it back to Union lines and eventually reached Washington. After treatment he returned to Detroit for a long period of recuperation.[41]

The First Michigan valiantly fought on until late afternoon, when McDowell's entire army began to fall back. The continual pressure of Confederate attacks and the lack of relief from fresh troops prevented the North from rallying. Finally, as one Light Guardsman remembered, the formal "command to retreat was given, and mournfully we took the flag and, gathering what men they [sic] could, joined in that terrible retreat." The regiment returned to the wooded area from which it had started in the early hours of that morning "in such high spirits." It had been such a long and fearful day that to the members of Company A and their comrades it must have seemed as if the late afternoon somehow were another age rather than another part of 21 July. After a brief respite, the battle-weary troops received orders to return to the District of Columbia.

> We started in order, but without a moment's halt, worn and tired, our poor fellows kept straggling out, and arrived in squads at Washington the following morning, having marched nearly sixty miles in twenty-four hours, without sleep, with no food but hard bread, and no drink but muddy water, and a little at that, for thirty-six hours. God knows the old regiment did what they could; cool and brave they went into that fight, and had they been properly supported would have cleared the field. . . . Nothing could have saved the retreat; we had neither the men nor the artillery to beat back those fresh troops of Johnston.[42]

One of the key Union commanders at Gettysburg said of the Wolverine State troops at the First Battle of Bull Run that "the 1st Michigan on the extreme right held the most advanced position we occupied that disastrous day." A leading student of Michigan in the Civil War reported: "A survey of the field after the battle discovered the fact that the Michigan dead were found nearest the enemy's works." The price for this bravery and dedication proved a distressing one; of the approximately five hundred men and officers who went into the fray on 21 July 1861, the First Michigan Regiment had suffered nearly one-third casualties.[43]

Despite their bitter defeat the regiment and the other Union troops in the area of the capital soon rallied and presented a formidable barrier to any Southern attack on Washington. But the reverse in that first major battle of the war in Virginia taught the Northerners the harsh lesson that the struggle to restore the Union would be both longer and more difficult than they had anticipated.[44] This understanding had immediate implications for the Light Guardsmen and their comrades of the First Michigan, which had been formed as a ninety-day regiment. The unit's term of enlistment expired in August 1861, but with the expectation of a prolonged war, many of the members of the group would choose to join a reconstituted three-year organization after the First had returned to the Wolverine State.[45]

The return of Michigan's three-month regiment to Detroit combined aspects of both a triumphal tour and a moving experience for the members of the First Michigan and the enthusiastic and grateful crowd who greeted them. On 2 August 1861 booming cannon, presumably fired with powder but not cannonballs, announced the homecoming of the regiment to Detroit. The warmth of the greeting by the townspeople more than matched the heat of an exceptionally hot August day. As the train chugged into the Detroit and Milwaukee Station, a great crush of Detroiters and outstate Michiganians, some of whom had been waiting five hours in temperatures that exceeded one hundred degrees, welcomed the returning veterans. The regimental band appropriately played "Home, Sweet Home," and, following the obligatory round of formal speeches by local notables, the crowd responded with "three roaring cheers" for the troops.[46]

The First Michigan was officially "mustered out of service August 7th, 1861." Its end as a three-month unit did not mark the termination of either the service of the Light Guard or of the regiment designated the First Michigan during the Civil War. The Light Guardsmen of Company A

overwhelmingly reenlisted in the three-year First Michigan. A few had suffered serious wounds or illnesses or were prevented from continuing in service by family difficulties. Some members of the Light Guard who had advanced in rank through the distinction of their ninety-day service utilized their special backgrounds by serving as key officers in other regiments. The main thrust of the Light Guard's activities during the Civil War, however, continued within the reorganized First Michigan.[47]

Indeed, it is by recounting the key experiences of the First Michigan in the remainder of the war that one can assess the contributions of the Light Guard in the struggle. Early in 1862 the First Michigan found itself "encamped at Annapolis Junction, Maryland, guarding the Washington and Baltimore Railroad." This line comprised a vital transportation link for the Union government and its army. Then in March the regiment became part of the garrison at Fortress Monroe, a crucial federal stronghold in northern Virginia.[48]

The year of 1862 can be characterized as one of rapidly changing fortunes between the Union and the Confederacy. The First Michigan took part in a number of encounters in the summer of that year, although full details of the grim catalog of engagements were not preserved. The sites of action included Mechanicsville, Gaines's Mill, Peach Orchard, Savage Station, Turkey Bend, White Oak Swamp, and Malvern Hill. "The part taken by the regiment in these battles was, unfortunately, not reported, although it is known to have been actively engaged, and to have served with efficiency and gallantry. Its losses were 35 killed and died of wounds, and 97 missing in action." The above battles, however, are usually thought of as part of the "Peninsula campaign." During that period the First Michigan was attached to the First Brigade, First Division, Fifth Corps, under George B. McClellan, who had placed his troops on the Yorktown Peninsula in Virginia, where they threatened Richmond. Robert E. Lee, with the aid of the particularly able Stonewall Jackson, struck back in the series of battles and skirmishes that involved the Wolverine troops.[49]

Later in the summer the First Brigade was transferred to the command of John Pope; under the leadership of that energetic but not always astute general, it engaged in the campaign that culminated at the end of August in the Second Battle of Bull Run or Manassas, which constituted another disaster for the Northern armies. In this 1862 struggle at Manassas, the Fifth Corps, which included the Michigan men, had the dubious distinction of serving under General Fitz-John Porter, one of the most controversial federal officers of the period, whose performance in the Union defeat would lead to his court-martial.[50]

In fairness to the First Michigan, its fellow Northern troops, and the officers who commanded them at the Second Battle of Bull Run, it must be said that they faced brilliant generalship on the part of Lee and Jackson. Lee had daringly divided his forces in the face of formidable Union opposition and dispatched "Jackson's corps on a wide flanking march around Pope's right to sever his supply line. In two days (August 25–26) Jackson's foot cavalry legged more than fifty miles to fall on the hugh Union supply depot at Manassas. . . . His hungry and footsore soldiers seized all the Union supplies they could eat or carry away and put the rest to the torch."[51]

General Pope decided to seize this opportunity to decimate Jackson's army before that wily commander could rejoin Lee's main force of Confederate troops. "Seldom has a general been more completely confused than Pope was now. He had vast energy, and he set his troops to marching back and forth to surround and destroy Jackson, but he could not quite find where Jackson was." Then, on 28 August, a unit of the federal army encountered the elusive Confederate leader. By dawn on 29 August a major battle had been joined in the vicinity of Bull Run, and once again the Northern forces were badly outmaneuvered by their Southern opponents. The Fifth Corps found itself hurled into the midst of the fight without adequate guidance to enable it to be effective. "Porter's corps came up on the Union left in a position to move against Jackson's flank, but having no specific orders and misled by a dust cloud that Stuart's cavalry kicked up to convince him that a strong body of infantry was in his front, Porter did nothing."[52]

In the midst of this confusion, a close student of the First Michigan recorded that

the regiment, in command of Colonel Roberts, was in . . . Porter's corps (5th), and had taken a position in some woods fronting the enemy's lines, and not far from one of his well posted and important batteries. The order was given to advance and dislodge the rebels and silence this battery, and at 4 P.M. the 1st Michigan, with the 13th New York and 18th Massachusetts regiments of infantry, deployed column and advancing, a terrific infantry fire from a force in ambush and five unseen batteries opening a cross-fire upon them with murderous effect, . . . fifty percent of the regiment were either killed or wounded. The men, under these trying circumstances, behaved coolly and with much bravery, standing their ground like veterans, and not until success became hopeless and the order to retreat was given did they fall back, and then in good order, when they resumed their former position in the woods, and reformed with their division. Had there been any possibility of victory under such circumstances, their courage and persistency would have secured it.

If both battles of Bull Run ended with severe reverses for the Union army, in neither case did the failure of Northern arms represent any want of daring or bravery on the part of troops such as the First Michigan. The Wolverine contingent, despite its efforts, found itself trapped in a distressing set of circumstances, including inadequate generalship, in the face of particularly shrewd and able foes.[53]

Next the First Michigan took part in the fierce and bloody battle at Antietam in September 1862, under the leadership of General McClellan. Lee's bold willingness to take unconventional risks as a general had produced such great success for the Southern cause in August 1862 that he decided to take his exhausted army, in which "food was low, [and] thousands of men were shoeless," and push them into a campaign against numerically superior Union forces. This strategy resulted in one of the most savage confrontations of the war, and one in which the First Michigan performed valuable yeoman service, resulting in heavy casualties for the regiment. The battle of Antietam has aptly been described as "gory beyond description." The fight began the evening of 16 September when McClellan moved part of his army across Antietam Creek and met enemy troops. The whole encounter produced a total of more than twenty-three

thousand casualties, nearly eight thousand of whom were killed immediately or later died of wounds. "By way of comparison: on D-Day in World War II, American forces suffered 6,000 casualties. . . . More than twice as many Americans were killed or mortally wounded in combat in a single day at Antietam as in the War of 1812, the Mexican War, and the Spanish-American War *combined.*" No wonder Antietam has earned the reputation as the bloodiest battle between the two armies—and, ironically, it was a draw.[54]

It was in a tactical sense that neither side secured an advantage over the other at Antietam. But in a strategic sense, in the long-run effect on the war, the September bloodbath led to a number of favorable consequences for the cause of the United States. Lee had hoped, when he marched into Maryland, that a successful Southern invasion of the North would encourage European governments and perhaps even the federal government to recognize the Confederacy. That desire had been frustrated by the rebel failure to defeat the Yankee forces at Antietam. Consequently, Lincoln, looking for favorable circumstances in which to issue the preliminary statement of the Emancipation Proclamation, did so five days after Antietam.[55]

Once again the general situation of the war was going to affect the nature of the leadership under which the First Michigan served. In late 1862 Lincoln lost patience with what he regarded as a lack of aggressiveness on the part of McClellan. On one occasion when the general protested that the cavalry horses in the Army of the Potomac had become much too tired to move, the president sarcastically inquired "what the horses of your army have done since the battle of Antietam that fatigues anything?" Early in November Lincoln removed McClellan from his command and gave the post to General Ambrose E. Burnside. The latter soon after contrived to attack the "united Confederate forces at Fredericksburg, where so great was the disadvantage of position that his preponderance of numbers was neutralized." The rebels had managed to place a good part of their forces in "an almost impregnable position. . . . Hopeless as was their plight, the Federals charged on with magnificent determination until at nightfall they retired, leaving the field strewn with their dead, which in many cases were piled three deep."[56]

During this valiant if vain attack, the members of the First Michigan fought with bravery and persistence. The commanding officer of the regiment, Colonel Abbott, recalled: "We were again in motion, leaving the main street, passing through a cross street to the left toward the battlefield, where we were exposed to a heavy fire from the enemy's batteries on the hill, killing and wounding many of our best and bravest men." At a later point in the struggle, he explained that "the regiment moved in line of battle to the front, and there commenced firing, which was continued at intervals until after dark. Captain Kennedy was mortally wounded while bravely leading his men. Here many of my best men were killed or wounded. Not an officer faltered; all exhibited the coolness and courage of veterans." In that dismal day of fruitless sacrifice at Fredericksburg, the First Michigan, which had already been engaged in costly campaigning for months, suffered nearly fifty additional casualties. Afterward, the regiment withdrew to a camp where its members rested and re-cuperated during the early winter months of 1863.[57]

Then in late April 1863 the Michiganians moved toward Chancellorsville to take part in yet another major battle. Lincoln, discouraged with Burnside's performance, had replaced him with Joseph Hooker. "Fighting Joe," a cavalry officer with the reputation of being an aggressive and daring commander in the field who fought as hard as he drank or courted the ladies, proved a good organizer for the Army of the Potomac. He described his command with his usual engaging modesty as "the finest army on the planet." Deciding to go on the offensive against the rebels, he clashed with the Army of Northern Virginia in the early days of May. Hooker's generalship, however, proved no match for Lee's, and the Union forces suffered heavy casualties, although the Confederates sustained an incalculable loss for their cause when, in the aftermath of the battle, the brilliant Stonewall Jackson was fatally shot by his own men, who mistook him for a Northern officer.[58]

At Chancellorsville Colonel Abbott recorded that the First Michigan's role had involved "a campaign which for all that tests the quality of a soldier surpasses all our former experience. Great credit is due both officers and men for the cheerfulness and fortitude with which they endured fatigue, hardship, and danger." The colonel concluded in his report: "We are proud of our State and proud of the reputation of Michigan troops. We sincerely trust that our future history will . . . give reason for faith in the hearts of the authorities and the people at home."[59]

Abbott, perhaps, had ended on such a plaintive note because of an understandable depression he and his fellow Northerners felt, since the victory they had so eagerly anticipated at Chancellorsville had turned into a bloody setback. The men of the Army of the Potomac, although subdued, did not lose confidence in themselves. Even then they sensed that the Southern success at Chancellorsville reflected not a lack of fighting skills on the part of the soldiers in blue but instead resulted from the fact that "Hooker's battlefield generalship was the worst of the war." Indeed, when Abraham Lincoln learned what Hooker had been able to do with "the finest army on the planet," the president is alleged to have said, "My God! my God! What will the country say?"[60]

The Northern public may have been discouraged after Chancellorsville, but it did not lose heart. The leaders of the Confederacy realized that they would have to win the kind of victory that would break the will of the Union supporters. Otherwise, the larger population and superior industrial resources of the North would eventually turn the tide of the struggle against the South. General Lee would have to chance taking his army north to try to strike a decisive blow against the federal government. Such a strategy entailed a high risk, for the rebels would lose the advantage of fighting on their home ground. The Army of Northern Virginia also lacked adequate supplies for invading enemy territory. Nevertheless, Lee decided to gamble and go on the offensive. The Confederate commander, in a complex set of movements, began to lead his troops northward in June 1863.[61]

In the meantime, the First Michigan had repaired to "its camping ground near Falmouth" for some rest. By the end of May the Wolverines were ready to be sent closer to possible theaters of battle. For them, as for so many other Union units, "the

month of June was occupied in marching and maneuvering." Soon they encountered the enemy. As Lee attempted to move into Union-held territory he made heavy use of Jeb Stuart's famous cavalry both for reconnoitering the opposition and for screening the movements of his own troops. In early June Northerners, trying to locate the main body of the Southern forces, "precipitated the largest cavalry battle of the war at Brandy Station, near Culpeper." In that engagement in Virginia, the First Michigan served as infantry support for federal mounted soldiers. After fighting all day, the Union men were forced back. During the clash, however, the Northern troops, including the Wolverines, had made an impressive showing against the rebels.[62]

Less than a month later, Union forces converged at Gettysburg, Pennsylvania, and prepared to repel Lee's invasion. The First Michigan "after laborious and exhausting marches under a broiling sun . . . reached Gettysburg, Pa., at 1.30 A.M. of July 2d." The Wolverines, who were still attached to the Fifth Army Corps, had arrived just in time to participate in the crucial Battle of Gettysburg. Late in the afternoon a Union advance left the hill Little Round Top undefended, and troops from the Fifth were ordered to take up station there. They managed to get to the hill only "minutes ahead of the charging Confederates." The most specific details of the First Michigan's notable performance come from the report of Lieutenant Colonel William A. Throop, who had taken charge of the First Michigan after Colonel Abbott had been wounded in the fighting:

On the morning of the 2d we were formed in line of battle, in reserve, where we remained until about 4 o'clock P.M., when we (with the brigade) were ordered to the front. We got into position in line about 4.30 P.M. . . . We had no sooner got our line fully established than the enemy drove in our skirmishers and appeared in force . . . within two hundred yards of our line. We ordered our men to fix bayonets, and commenced firing on the enemy with a deadly effect, driving him back after a severe fire of half an hour. He, however, soon returned, and was a second time driven back with great loss. Our men stood up bravely under the storm of bullets sent against them, loading and firing as coolly as though on drill. . . . Our color-bearer . . . was the first man wounded after the firing commenced. The colors were at once taken from the ground . . . and gallantly borne through the battle. . . . We maintained our line, repulsing and holding in check the enemy until 7.30 P.M., when we were ordered to fall back. . . . Men never behaved more gallantly than did the soldiers of the 1st Michigan in this battle, and it would be impossible to mention each case of individual gallantry and bravery when all did so well.

The Wolverine regiment, which entered the Battle of Gettysburg with 145 officers and men, suffered 44 casualties in that struggle.[63]

Though the Union armies as a whole, like the First Michigan, sustained fearful losses at Gettysburg in those days of furious fighting from 1 to 3 July 1863, they had turned the tide of the war. Under the leadership of General George Gordon Meade they had repulsed Lee's desperate attempt to save the faltering Confederate cause by invading the North. There would still be a long road for the blue-clad federals, including the Michiganians, to follow, however, for Lee was able to escape with the main part of his army. In the subsequent campaigning during the nearly two years of war that remained, the Light Guard, as part of the First Michigan, would continue to participate in key and deadly battles.[64]

In the last months of 1863 the Wolverines did a good deal of marching and maneuvering and engaged in a number of smaller, but important, conflicts for the Union cause. As winter approached the unit's activities increasingly became confined to "picket and guard duty" on the Orange and Alexandria Railroad in Virginia. The First Michigan's three-year term ended in February, and a large percentage of its members "re-enlisted as veterans." The regiment then "was ordered to report at Detroit, Michigan, where it arrived on the 1st of March, and was furloughed for thirty days." The First Michigan returned to the front early in April. This reenlisting of a substantial part of a seasoned group was tremendously important. Even after the success of 1863 the Union would still face great difficulties. It was necessary for the federal army to retain the best of its three-year veterans because "morale among front-line Confederate troops remained high, aided by a wave of religious revivals in the winter camps." The rebel army, for a complex set of reasons, found it easier to retain experienced soldiers. Consequently, regiments such as the First Michigan, with a high percentage of battle-wise men, played an important role in the awesome and decisive struggle that ultimately led to the Union triumph at Appomattox. And Detroit's Light Guardsmen continued to serve with distinction in the campaign to preserve the United States.[65]

The crucial events of 1864 began with the grim Battle of the Wilderness in May. In March of that year Lincoln selected Ulysses S. Grant, who had proven himself one of the most capable of federal officers in the fighting in the West, to be "general in chief" of the Union army with the title of lieutenant general. "Congress had revived the rank, . . . previously held only by George Washington." The only other officer to hold this designation, Winfield Scott, had it "by brevet only." After arriving in the capital, Grant decided that he "had no intention of becoming a desk general. He thenceforth made his headquarters with the Army of the Potomac, becoming in effect its strategic field commander while Meade remained its titular and tactical commander."[66]

When the First Michigan returned from its month's furlough in April, it soon became involved in the strenuous campaigning and bloodletting that stemmed from Grant's relentless pursuit of rebel forces. The new general in chief's strategy was not conquering land but destroying Confederate military strength. "'Lee's army will be your objective point,' Grant told Meade. 'Wherever Lee goes, there you will go also.'" In the fighting that ensued, the First Michigan remainder under the command of Colonel Throop, and it continued in the Fifth Corps of the Army of the Potomac; however, by the spring of 1864, the regiment had been attached to the Third rather than the First Brigade of the First Division.[67]

Throop and the Wolverines were with the Union troops as they began to pour across the Rapidan River into Virginia to seek out Lee. The wily Southerner, however, so maneuvered his army that the Northerners would have to attack in the area of unkempt, uncultivated terrain called "the Wilderness," where the rebels had "brought Joe Hooker to grief exactly one year earlier in the battle of Chancellorsville." The entry of the federal soldiers into the Wilderness was not propitious. Either animals or erosion had uncovered the shallow graves of Northern troops killed in the previous struggle, and both veterans and fresh recruits in the Army of the Potomac must have been chilled at the sight of the numerous skeletons of their predecessors scattered throughout the desolate area.[68]

"Grant had hoped to get through the Wilderness into clear country before giving battle," but Lee's astute tactics prevented him from doing so. In some particularly savage fighting on 5 May both armies sustained horrendous casualties—a total of twenty-eight thousand men, nearly 20 percent of the forces involved. So great were their losses that the Union soldiers at first thought that they had suffered yet another disaster. They feared they would recross the Rapidan in shame. In Grant, however, the Yankees had a commander whose belligerent instincts and willingness to do battle matched if not exceeded Lee's. Thus, "when night fell and the men received orders to march *south*, the realization suddenly dawned that whether the Wilderness had been a victory or a defeat, this army was no longer going to retreat. Even though they had just been through hell and the move southward promised more hell, the smoke-grimed Yanks felt a sense of elation." The members of the Army of the Potomac felt almost exuberant as they realized they followed a leader at last willing to battle toe to toe with the bellicose rebel commanders.[69]

Colonel Throop's reports on his unit in that period included in pride rather than sorrow the observation, "*For eight successive days, we were either in a fight or skirmish.*" This service involved constant casualties for the First Michigan. Indeed, the colonel fairly commented, "Our work has been very severe, marching and fighting continually."[70]

As his army struggled southward from the Wilderness, Grant's goal centered around a point called Spotsylvania Courthouse. The beleaguered grey-clad followers of Lee skillfully entrenched themselves in this area; some Civil War battles were beginning to approximate the trench warfare of the First World War more than half a century later. In particular, at a salient in the Confederate lines that came to be known as the "'Bloody Angle,'... some of the most savage fighting of the war took place.... Fighting madness turned men into killing machines." One officer spoke for countless participants in the bloodbath when he recorded, "I never expect to be fully believed when I tell what I saw of the horrors of Spotsylvania." It was during this episode at Spotsylvania that Ulysses S. Grant issued his famous pledge "to fight it out on this line if it takes all summer."[71]

Grant continued to press Lee. The battle was soon joined again at "a dusty, desolate crossroads known as Cold Harbor." The area had received its distinctive name "because the tavern there provided drink and overnight accommodations but no hot meals." The soldiers of the Army of the Potomac, including the First Michigan, went into combat against the well-fortified Southern troops with dogged courage. The Northerners had no illusions about their chances of not surviving under such circumstances; on the eve of the struggle "many of them pinned slips of paper with name and address on their coats so their bodies could be identified after the battle." The onslaught on Cold Harbor proved as unsuccessful as it was bloody. The Union army suffered seven thousand casualties, "most of them in the first few minutes" of the attack on the virtually impregnable Confederate fortifications. Grant later expressed great regret for having ordered this particular action.[72]

Grant, however, did not lose his nerve after the horrible losses at Cold Harbor. He swiftly and skillfully moved his army across the bridgeless James River. Soon the Northern troops "were surging against the defenses of Petersburg." The Light Guardsmen and their comrades of the First Michigan found themselves engaged in another large-scale and costly struggle. Petersburg represented a key point. Its capture might not only force the Confederate capital of Richmond to capitulate but also enable Grant to trap Lee's Army of Northern Virginia. The Southern soldiers, however, had time to use what was becoming the most effective rebel tool of the war, the spade, and they were able to place themselves in an effective network of trenches. This well-defended position proved too formidable for the federal troops to overwhelm. Having suffered over sixty thousand casualties since the beginning of the Wilderness campaign, "the Army of the Potomac [had lost] its fighting edge." Grant had originally hoped to move swiftly to strike a decisive blow against the enemy, but Lee's skill had frustrated the Union leader's desire for a quick victory, and soon the action at Petersburg settled into precisely the kind of prolonged and draining siege the Northern commander had wished to avoid.[73]

In the long investment of Petersburg the First Michigan took part in the fighting from the very start. "We crossed the James river on transports on the morning of the 16th," the regiment's commander recalled, "and marched directly for Petersburg, arriving before the city about daylight of the 17th." The Wolverines became involved in action on 18 June, and, according to a leading student of Michigan in the war, "From this date to the 17th of August, when it was relieved, the regiment was engaged in the construction of fortifications and in the trenches in front of Petersburg. The weather being exceedingly warm and the labor very great, the hardships which the regiment endured during this period were very severe. The men in the trenches were obliged to keep under cover to protect themselves from the enemy's artillery and the constant fire of sharpshooters."[74]

The prolonged fighting seemed to be leading to an impasse when Grant became interested in a special tactic. A Union soldier who had been a Pennsylvania miner suggested, "We could blow that damned fort out of existence if we could run a mine shaft under it." When some of the commanding general's staff called this idea to his attention, Grant was at first dubious of its practicality. With information supplied by engineers, however, his officers finally persuaded Grant of the possibility of undermining the Confederate lines with explosives and blowing up a large segment of the enemy's defense. The procedure was followed. Four tons of powder were detonated before dawn on 30 July with devastating effect on the Southern defenders and their fortifications. "As huge masses of earth shot into the air, 'men, guns, carriages, and timbers' were hurled aloft and buried in a shapeless ruin."[75]

Although the explosion resulted in a huge crater that broke the Southern line, confusion in Union leadership prevented the Northerners from successfully utilizing their opportunity. General Burnside, "a New Englander with antislavery sympathies, decided to give his black division special assault training to lead the attack." These troops enthusiastically devoted themselves to preparing for this dangerous and difficult assignment. At the last minute, however, it was decided to replace these black fighting men with white troops, who lacked the necessary expertise for the operation. Although ostensibly the change had been made to obviate the charge that white generals had used black soldiers for cannon fodder, it is more likely that the decision reflected a lack of faith in the reliability of the blacks despite the excellent record they had compiled in the Union army. "Old prejudices died hard," aptly comments a present-day scholar.[76]

The result of this last-minute alteration, whatever the reason for it, led to a tragically disorganized offensive. Many Northern troops rushed into the crater caused by the explosion "instead of fanning out right and left," and soon these attacking federals became trapped in the hole, making shockingly easy targets for rebel marksmen. Thus the Battle of the Crater proved to be a disaster. The failure, however, involved inadequate leadership at a high level rather than poor performance by the men and officers engaged in the operation.[77]

Although Grant was not able quickly to conquer Petersburg, he did keep the Army of Northern Virginia pinned down there, facilitating the success of Union armies in other areas, such as General Sherman's famous march to the sea through Georgia. As the winter of 1864–65 blended into spring, Grant determined to bring final victory to the Union cause. In the last drive against the faltering but still struggling rebels, the First Michigan served valiantly time and time again. It fought in episodes no longer memorable enough to survive readily in the public recollection but which were essential milestones on the hard path to victory. These included such engagements as the battles of Hatcher's Run, White Oak Road, Five Forks, and Amelia Court House. And the regiment took part in an event that does stand out boldly in the national memory: Lee's surrender of the Army of Northern Virginia to Grant at the McLean house in the village of Appomattox Courthouse on 9 April 1865.[78]

It had been a long, difficult road since April 1861 for all of those who supported the preservation of the United States of America. Soldiers from the Wolverine State, particularly the Light Guardsmen and their comrades of the First Michigan, had campaigned with great distinction. This was true of Detroit's Light Guard when its membership enlisted in the three-month regiment in the spring and summer of 1861, when its veterans served in the regiment's reincarnation as a three-year unit at the end of that summer, and when the

battle-scarred men once again gallantly reenlisted to continue to fight during the last fierce year of the struggle. The Light Guard played a valuable and courageous role in the war to preserve the Union.

After Lee's surrender the regiment sailed to Alexandria, Virginia, and subsequently traveled by railroad to Louisville, Kentucky. The First Michigan then camped at nearby Jeffersonville, Indiana. It was there that the regiment was formally mustered out of service. The men, however, returned to Michigan in a body, arriving home on 12 July 1865. As they hurried home, the Light Guardsmen and their comrades must have had some bittersweet thoughts about ending their long, difficult, and honorable association. They could be proud of their service to their country in such a dangerous ordeal. The Wolverine veterans must have had melancholy memories about those who did not return or who had suffered debilitating wounds. Of the 1,346 men who served in the three-year First Michigan Regiment, 243 had become casualties.[79]

Notes

1. *Detroit Free Press*, 9, 13 Jan., 20 Feb. 1861, in Helen H. Ellis, comp., *Michigan in the Civil War: A Guide to the Material in Detroit Newspapers 1861–1866* (Lansing, Mich., 1965), 1; George S. May, *Michigan and the Civil War Years, 1860–1866: A Wartime Chronicle* (Lansing, Mich., 1964), 4.

2. J. G. Randall and David Donald, *The Civil War and Reconstruction*, 2d ed. (Boston, 1961), 177; James M. McPherson, *Ordeal by Fire: The Civil War and Reconstruction* (New York, 1982), 145.

3. Frank B. Woodford, *Father Abraham's Children: Michigan Episodes in the Civil War* (Detroit, 1961), 21–23; *Detroit Free Press*, 16 Apr. 1861, in Ellis, 2.

4. Isham, Purcell, and Hogan, 26.

5. Ibid., 26, 29.

6. John Robertson, *Michigan in the War* (Lansing, Mich., 1882), 110.

7. Woodford, 41–42; Robertson, *Michigan*, 166, 966; G. May, 9; *Detroit Daily Advertiser*, 25 Apr. 1861, in Ellis, 5.

8. *Detroit Free Press*, 3 May 1861, in Ellis, 8.

9. *Detroit Daily Advertiser,* 6 May 1861; and *Detroit Free Press,* 7 May 1861, in Ellis, 9; Isham, Purcell, and Hogan, 29–33.

10. Isham, Purcell, and Hogan, 33–35.

11. Ibid., 36; *Detroit Daily Tribune,* 11 May 1861, and *Detroit Free Press,* 12 May 1861, in Ellis, 10.

12. *Detroit Free Press,* 11, 12 May 1861, in Ellis, 10; Isham, Purcell, and Hogan, 37.

13. Isham, Purcell, and Hogan, 38.

14. Ibid., 39; *Detroit Free Press,* 16 May 1861, in Ellis, 11.

15. Isham, Purcell, and Hogan, 39.

16. Ibid., 39, 41.

17. Ibid., 41; Woodford, 34.

18. Woodford, 34.

19. Clowes, 39; Isham, Purcell, and Hogan, 41; Robertson, *Michigan,* 168; Woodford, 34.

20. Woodford, 34–35.

21. Robertson, *Michigan,* 169. Although Lincoln's statement has never been clearly verified, as a leading historian of Michigan in the Civil War has pointed out, the quotation has been so widely circulated that it has become an integral part of Michigan lore. "And it is by no means unlikely that Lincoln did utter those words, or something very similar to them" (Woodford, 35, 260).

22. *Detroit Daily Advertiser,* 23 May 1861, in Woodford, 260; Isham, Purcell, and Hogan, 42; Clowes, 39–40.

23. Benjamin P. Thomas, *Abraham Lincoln: A Biography* (New York, 1952), 269.

24. Ibid., 269–70; Clowes, 40.

25. Robertson, *Michigan,* 169; Woodford, 38–39; Isham, Purcell, and Hogan, 43; Clowes, 40–41.

26. Woodford, 39–40; Isham, Purcell, and Hogan, 43.

27. Isham, Purcell, and Hogan, 43–44; Clowes, 42.

28. Isham, Purcell, and Hogan, 43–47; Woodford, 40.

29. Isham, Purcell, and Hogan, 44–45; Clowes, 42–43.

30. Isham, Purcell, and Hogan, 47.

31. Clowes, 43; McPherson, 163; Thomas, 273.

32. Clowes, 42–44.

33. McPherson, 206.

34. McPherson, 207; Clowes, 43.

35. McPherson, 207; Isham, Purcell, and Hogan, 48; Thomas, 271.

36. McPherson, 207; Thomas, 271.

37. McPherson, 208–10; Thomas, 271; Randall and Donald, 199.

38. Isham, Purcell, and Hogan, 48; Robertson, *Michigan,* 170; Clowes, 44–45.

39. Isham, Purcell, and Hogan, 49–52; Robertson, *Michigan,* 170–72.

40. Robertson, *Michigan,* 170–72; Woodford, 45–46.

41. Isham, Purcell, and Hogan, 54–55.

42. Ibid., 53.

43. Robertson, *Michigan,* 171–73.

44. McPherson, 210–11; Randall and Donald, 200.

45. Clowes, 53–55.

46. Isham, Purcell, and Hogan, 60–65; Clowes, 53–55.

47. Isham, Purcell, and Hogan, 67; Woodford, 50–51; Robertson, *Michigan,* 173.

48. Robertson, *Michigan,* 175.

49. Ibid.; Bruce Catton, *The American Heritage Short History of the Civil War* (New York, 1963), 63–68; Randall and Donald, 210–16.

50. Robertson, *Michigan,* 175; McPherson, 256–57.

51. McPherson, 255–56.

52. Catton, 88; McPherson, 256–57.

53. Robertson, *Michigan,* 175.

54. G. May, 35; McPherson, 280–85; Randall and Donald, 221.

55. Catton, 95–96, 105–6; McPherson, 288; Randall and Donald, 221.

56. Randall and Donald, 224–25.

57. Robertson, *Michigan,* 177.

58. Ibid.; Randall and Donald, 226, 399–401; McPherson, 319–23.

59. Robertson, *Michigan,* 177–79.

60. McPherson, 323.

61. Randall and Donald, 401; McPherson, 324; Catton, 131–32.

62. Robertson, *Michigan,* 179; Randall and Donald, 401; McPherson, 325.

63. Robertson, *Michigan,* 179–80; McPherson, 326–31.

64. Robertson, *Michigan,* 180–85; McPherson, 331–32.

65. Robertson, *Michigan,* 180–81; McPherson, 409–10.

66. McPherson, 410.

67. Robertson, *Michigan,* 181; McPherson, 411.

68. McPherson, 414–15.

69. Randall and Donald, 419; McPherson, 415–16.

70. Robertson, *Michigan,* 181.

71. McPherson, 416–20; Randall and Donald, 419.

72. McPherson, 420–22.

73. Randall and Donald, 421–23; McPherson, 422–26.

74. Robertson, *Michigan,* 182–83.

75. McPherson, 427; Randall and Donald, 423–24.

76. McPherson, 427.

77. McPherson, 427–28; Woodford, 198.

78. Robertson, *Michigan,* 185; McPherson, 482; Randall and Donald, 526–27.

79. Robertson, *Michigan,* 186.

Late Nineteenth Century

After the Civil War Americans became preoccupied with the internal development of the country, and interest in military affairs greatly decreased. The members of the Light Guard, however, continued its traditions as the senior militia company and a volunteer organization regarded by many as one of the finest west of the Appalachian Mountains and "Detroit's own." In early December 1865 the unit's Board of Direction resolved: "All those who were mustered into the U.S. Service as Members of Company 'A' of the First Michigan Infantry . . . who were not active members previously of the Guard be and are declared to have been members of the Detroit Light Guard from the date they were so mustered into such service."[1]

By the beginning of 1866, then, soldiers coming back from the Civil War added to the vigor of the group that a later observer proudly designated the "veteran company not only of this city, but of Michigan." In the late nineteenth century the citizen-soldiers returned to the concerns and pursuits that had occupied them before 1861. The militia endeavored to attract a steady stream of recruits who were able to meet the exacting physical, moral, and intellectual standards of the Light Guard. The exchange of visits with other volunteer military units also engaged its attention, as did drawing up the plans to construct a new building to replace their facilities for training "in the old Firemen's Hall." This preparation would culminate in the completion of the armory at the corner of Brush and Larned in 1898.[2]

The organization, while continuing to emphasize military affairs, performed numerous civic duties ranging from appearing at the cornerstone-laying ceremony for the new State Capitol in 1873 to serving as part of the honor guard at the funeral in Cleveland of President James A. Garfield in

1881. On the latter occasion the Light Guard had been chosen to join a number of other special militia groups as well as units of the regular army in making a "procession, four miles in length" that accompanied the body of the late chief executive to the cemetery. Referring to all of the troops who came from Michigan, one Cleveland paper cited the Detroit Light Guard as "the senior and the best drilled company of the battalion."[3]

The Light Guard played such a distinctive role in the history of Detroit that its importance in the community gave it virtually an official standing. Indeed, for a time, the city considered giving the company an annual subsidy, but for a variety of technical reasons, especially the reluctance of municipal leaders to consider more junior militia units for the same treatment, the proposal was dropped. By the 1870s a number of members who had been active in the senior group of citizen-soldiers reached an age at which it became difficult for them to serve in an active role. These individuals nevertheless wished to continue their association with the Light Guard. As a result, they decided to form a Veteran Corps for those no longer engaged in training but wishing to share their knowledge with a newer generation of recruits. In December 1877, therefore, under the leadership of such men as Colonel Lum, who had served in the Civil War, a group of twenty veterans, including several who had signed the original pledge to reorganize the militia under the name Detroit Light Guard on 16 November 1855, agreed to work toward the formation of a Veteran Corps to serve as an auxiliary branch of the company.[4]

The actual establishment of this group awaited the silver anniversary year of the Light Guard in 1880. The special celebration held by Detroit's oldest militia unit on this occasion affirmed that the membership would preserve its history. The local press coverage of the parade marking the company's twenty-fifth birthday paid deference to the emblem that the Detroit Light Guard had informally adopted by boldly heading the story, "THE TIGERS!" The members of the unit were accompanied on that special occasion not only by three bands but also by representatives of younger militia organizations in the area. One of these, an offshoot, the Detroit Light Infantry, had an especially poignant relationship to the Detroit Light Guard.[5]

In June 1877 dissidents had broken away from Detroit's senior militia group over policy differences, whose significance have long since vanished, but which had become intensified by personality clashes. These individuals, who did not want the company to continue in state service, had become known as the Secession Light Guard. These "secessionists" attempted to gain control of the name, assets, and records of the Detroit Light Guard. The remaining members of the volunteer militia prevented this in court in April 1878, and at that time the discontented faction took the name Detroit Light Infantry. In 1880, however, acrimonious feelings between the two groups had subsided sufficiently that the rebel company was pleased to honor the older band of citizen-soldiers. Despite some strains between the two over the next generation, the secessionists, attracted by the values and traditions of the Light Guard, rejoined it toward the end of the first decade of the twentieth century, although the formal consolidation of the two groups did not take place until 1911.[6]

In the silver anniversary parade, "the bracing wind bore the strains of music with the cheers of the populace, while flags and banners fluttered in the air." During the festivities of the day, notable events included the participation in the marching by thirty-eight members of the Veteran Corps, who had been "provided with blue caps and handsome blue badges, . . . with Oliver Goldsmith as the bearer of the old Williams' Flag, which has been the property of the company for many years. This flag, or banner, bears a portrait of the late Gen. Williams, which was painted by Col. Chas. M. Lum, also one of the first commanding officers of the company." On that day a number of civic-minded women presented the Light Guard with a new flag "of the heaviest silk, red and white stripes and a blue field which bears a striking facsimile of a tiger's head, hand-worked with silk embroidery in such a way that the head stands out very prominent on the field. . . . The flag was made by Horsman Brothers & Co., of Philadelphia, who copied the head from a large tiger in the Zoological Gardens." Upon receiving the gift, the Light Guard cheered, "'T-i-g-e-r! Whizz-zz! Boom! A-h-h!' . . . given with a will." Although not officially adopted on the crest until 1 May 1882, the tiger's head had been used by the company at least as far back as 1878.[7]

The spirit of the day and the worthiness of the traditions of the militia were eloquently expressed by a speaker at the banquet concluding the festivities. He asserted that "there was nothing more noble in the country than the citizen-soldiery" and proudly recalled the departure to the front in 1861 of the "volunteer army" trained in "this nursery of soldiers—the Detroit Light Guard." That the membership would continue to support the organization was expressed in the convictions of another speaker of the evening who declared that "the hope of a great free nation lay in its militia."[8]

In the years after the Civil War a great deal of the energy of the Light Guard's leadership was devoted to obtaining recruits who would be not only devoted soldiers but also gentlemen. Such gentlemen were not defined in the narrow class sense, but rather they were individuals who would have natural and instinctive qualities of decency and responsibility. The minutes of the organization reveal a preoccupation with securing volunteers who would "raise the Company up to a high standard."[9]

Although the Light Guard on the whole attracted individuals of superior quality to its ranks, at times some found it difficult to meet the obligations of the citizen-soldier. The two leading reasons for either expulsion or resignation from the militia involved non-payment of dues or failure to turn out regularly for training. Such lapses stemmed from the variety of economic circumstances and vocational situations from which the membership was drawn. "Being unable to attend drills and give the attention to the active corps that I should, I hereby tender my resignation," was the explanation of a committed citizen-soldier who found the responsibilities of making a living incompatible with his civic impulses. In a similar fashion another guardsman had to ask to leave the service averring, "I am employed on the street cars and am working nights. It will be impossible for me to attend any drills for 1 or 2 years." Difficult economic times also prevented some members from meeting their financial obligations, such as the individual who explained, "I find it impossible to pay dues as I have been out of work for some time." A few men were not always so conscientious in facing their inability to carry out their duties and had to be dismissed from the militia by disciplinary action.[10]

At times, cases involving defects in character or the inability to control exuberant spirits had to be brought before the Light Guard's board. Individuals were warned to take care so that in the future "conditions as regards sobriety could not be questioned." The organization would not tolerate conduct such as that of a guardsman who entered the armory "in an intoxicated condition" and then "picked fights" and finally went to sleep in a "water closet." More awkward was the report of a member of the House Committee that "complaint was made to me by a member of the Harmonie, during a Hop given by that Society . . . that Mr. H . . . and a lady (?) were drinking beer in the room known as the 'Quarter Master's Dept.' I saw the beer taken into the room and I went up to ask Mr. H . . . for an explanation. I found the door locked." Such embarrassing incidents, to be sure, were infrequent and minor episodes in the militia's history.[11]

The Detroit Light Guard, as the senior military unit of Michigan's city upon the straits, continued as a bulwark of community stability. Symbolically, the organization had laid the cornerstone for its Brush Street Armory in 1897, just a year before having to face the most severe challenge to the United States armed forces since the outbreak of the Civil War. The Light Guard would once again come forward to perform its duty in the defense of the United States.

Notes

1. Clowes, 54–73; *Detroit Free Press*, 17 Nov. 1880; "Brief History of the 425th Infantry Regiment," Ford D. McParland Papers, Collection of Detroit Armory Corporation (hereafter cited as DAC), mimeo; Record of the Proceedings of the Board of Direction, 28 Dec. 1865, Detroit Light Guard Minutes, vol. 2, 1860–71, BHC.

2. *Detroit Free Press*, 17 Nov. 1886, 17 Nov. 1880; Clowes, 57–58, 80–82; Robert B. Ross, *Landmarks of Detroit* (Detroit, 1898), 588; Detroit Public Library, *Detroit in Its World Setting* (Detroit, 1953), 186.

3. Record of the Company Meeting, 1 Sept. 1873, Detroit Light Guard Minutes, vol. 3, 1872–88, 22, BHC; Margaret Leech and Harry J. Brown, *The Garfield Orbit* (New York, 1978), 248; *Cleveland Herald Leader*, 27 Sept. 1881; Detroit Light Guard Minutes, 3:161, BHC.

4. Record of the Proceedings of the Board of Direction, 16 Mar. 1868, Detroit Light Guard Minutes, vol 2, 1860–71, BHC; Record of the Company Meeting, 4 May 1868, ibid.; 1 Oct. 1877, ibid., 3:82; 3 Dec. 1877, ibid., 3:85; The Original Call of the Detroit Light Guard, Veteran Corps, Selections, R2 Record Book, 1880–1908, 1–3, BHC; Clowes, 24–25, 365–67; Isham, Purcell, and Hogan, 87.

5. Clowes, 365–67; Isham, Purcell, and Hogan, 87; Detroit Light Guard, Veteran Corps, Selections, R2 Record Book, 1880–1908, 3–7, BHC; *Detroit Free Press*, 17 Nov. 1880.

6. Clowes, 61; Isham, Purcell, and Hogan, 85–86; Record of the Company Meeting, 4 June 1877, Detroit Light Guard Minutes, 3:69, BHC; ibid., 25 June 1887, 3:70–71; ibid., 26 June 1887, 3:72–74; ibid., 9 July 1887, 3:76; ibid., 6 Aug. 1887, 3:77–78; ibid., 4 Feb. 1878, 3:92; ibid., 8 Apr. 1878, 3:98–99; Minutes of Company Meeting, 25 June 1877, Detroit Light Infantry Minutes, vol. 1, 1887–89, 16, BHC; ibid., 8 Apr. 1878, 1:35–36; Minutes of Annual Meeting, 5 Dec. 1910, Detroit Light Infantry Minutes, vol. 2, 1890–1908 [i.e., 1911]; Minutes of Adjourned Annual Meeting, 9 Jan. 1911, ibid.

7. *Detroit Free Press,* 17 Nov. 1880; *Detroit Evening Telegraph,* 23 Feb. 1878.

8. *Detroit Free Press,* 17 Nov. 1880.

9. Record of the Proceedings of the Board of Direction, 2 Mar. 1868, Detroit Light Guard Minutes, vol. 2, 1860–71, BHC; Record of the Company Meeting, 6 Mar. 1871, ibid.

10. Frank J. Durling to Charles W. Harrah, 4 Nov. 1896, Detroit Light Guard Papers, Manuscript Box 1, BHC; Edward Bateson to J. W. Steiner, 21 Mar. 1896, ibid.; Turner Stanton to Detroit Light Guard Board of Directors, 26 Jan. 1895, ibid.

11. Statement of Board of Directors, 6 Oct. 1897, Detroit Light Guard Papers, Manuscript Box 1, BHC; File of Disciplinary Reports, 1897, ibid.; George H. Fuller to Board of Directors, 1 Apr. 1896, ibid.

Alpheus S. Williams as a major general, circa 1865. (Courtesy of the Burton Historical Collection, Detroit Public Library.)

Regimental National Colors of the First Michigan Regiment during the Civil War. (Courtesy of the photographer, H. J. Bell, Lansing, and the State Archives of Michigan.)

Colonel Horace Smith Roberts as commander of the First Michigan, 1862. Colonel Roberts was killed at the Second Battle of Bull Run. Photographic restoration by Frank E. Storer. (Courtesy of the Burton Historical Collection, Detroit Public Library.)

"D. L. I. Quick-Step," the cover to sheet music of a popular tune of the 1880s. Cover: Calvert Lithograph Company. (Courtesy of the 225th Infantry Archives.)

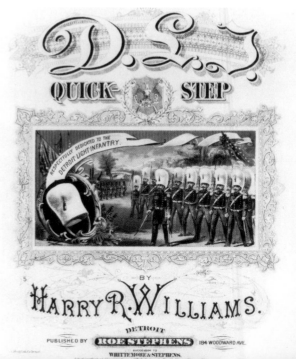

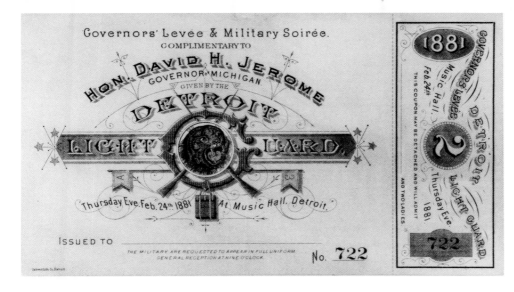

Ticket to a ball in honor of the governor of Michigan in 1881. The Light Guard held many major social events in the late nineteenth century. Photographer: Frank E. Storer. (Courtesy of the 225th Infantry Archives.)

Noncommissioned officers, Company A, Detroit Light Guard, circa 1872. Photographer: James A. Brush. (Courtesy of the Detroit Historical Museum.)

Firemen's Hall at Jefferson Avenue and Randolph Street in 1881. The Detroit Light Guard rented rooms here before it built its own armory at Larned and Brush. (Courtesy of the Burton Historical Collection, Detroit Public Library.)

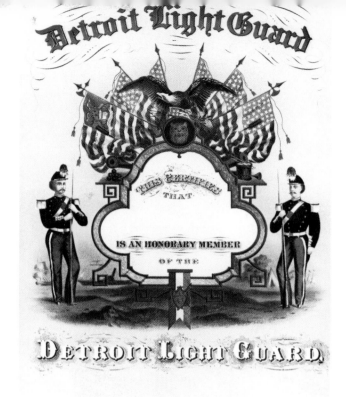

Officers of the Detroit Light Guard, circa 1882. Captain A. P. T. Beniteau is in the center. (Courtesy of the Detroit Historical Museum.)

Certificate of honorary membership awarded to citizens who supported the Detroit Light Guard, circa 1881. Artist: Calvert Lithograph Company. (Courtesy of the Frank E. Storer Collection.)

The Detroit City Greys in Milwaukee, Wisconsin, in 1884. The company was commanded by Captain Martin G. Borgman (prone, left front), and First Lieutenant was C. Ed Richmond. In June 1890 the Greys amalgamated with the Detroit Light Guard, becoming Company F. Photographer: Sutter, Milwaukee. (Courtesy of the Detroit Historical Museum.)

John Pallisore in the dress uniform of the Detroit Light Infantry, circa 1890. Photographer: C. M. Hayes & Company. (Courtesy of the Detroit Historical Museum.)

Reception room in the J. J. Bagley Memorial Armory of the Detroit Light Infantry on Congress Street, built in 1886. (Courtesy of the Detroit Historical Museum, George Winckler Collection.)

Noncommissioned officers of Company A, Detroit Light Guard, circa 1890. Corporal John S. Bersey (left rear) was later adjutant general of Michigan. (Courtesy of the 225th Infantry Archives and the Bersey Family.)

Parade of the Grand Army of the Republic, the leading organization of Union war veterans, passing City Hall and the Soldiers and Sailors Monument in Detroit in 1891. (Courtesy of the Detroit Historical Museum.)

Detroit Light Guard Band and the Fourth Infantry leaving for Bay City, Michigan, to join in a Fourth of July celebration in 1892. (Courtesy of the Detroit Historical Museum.)

Company A, Fourth Michigan State Troops, in dress uniform, circa 1892. Photographer: Alvord & Company. (Courtesy of the Detroit Historical Museum.)

John S. Bersey in the uniform of a regimental sergeant major of the Fourth Infantry in October 1894. Photographer: C. M. Hayes & Company. (Courtesy of the 225th Infantry Archives.)

Officers of the Detroit Light Infantry at Camp Rich, Island Lake, Michigan, in 1894. The first man on the left in the second row was the chaplain of the Detroit Light Guard. Photographer: W. H. Gardiner. (Courtesy of the Detroit Historical Museum.)

Ground breaking ceremony for the Light Guard Armory at Larned and Brush, 31 May 1897. Colonel Charles M. Lum lifted the first shovel of earth. Photographer: Charles L. Major. (Courtesy of the 225th Infantry Archives.)

St. John's and Harris Cadets in Pontiac after they had marched from Detroit, 20 August 1892. St. John's Cadets consolidated with the Detroit Light Guard on 9 January 1896, becoming Company M. (Courtesy of the Detroit Historical Museum from M. W. Dickenson #62.283.1.)

Invocation at the laying of the cornerstone of the Light Guard Armory, 18 October 1897. (Courtesy of the 225th Infantry Archives.)

Spanish-American War

In the generation after the Civil War the status of the island of Cuba, barely ninety miles off the coast of Florida, became an issue of increasing concern for Americans. Even after most of Spain's colonies in the Western Hemisphere had successfully rebelled and established their independence, Cuba remained part of the Spanish empire and suffered greatly from poor administration and economic exploitation. Periodic uprisings by the island's people culminated in the rebellion of 1895, which led to a long period of often brutal warfare between imperial troops and local inhabitants. The press of the United States thoroughly covered the events, and Americans overwhelmingly sympathized with the insurgents, as the native rebels were called. Particularly upsetting to United States citizens were reports of "reconcentration camps" into which many farmers and their families were herded to prevent them from giving any aid to the opponents of the Spanish authorities. William McKinley entered the White House in March 1897. A Civil War veteran with a distinguished combat record, the new president was nevertheless deeply committed to maintaining peace with Spain if it could be done without violating national honor.[1]

The development of disorders in Havana early in 1898 finally led McKinley to dispatch the battleship *Maine* to Cuban waters to protect the United States citizens living there, if necessary. Tragically, however, on 15 February an explosion destroyed this warship while it was in Havana harbor, and aides awakened the president early the next morning to inform him of the disaster. At the end of March a United States board of inquiry reported that the *Maine* had been sunk as the result of an external explosion but made no attempt to ascertain responsibility for it. Long before this official statement, however, the public had furiously blamed the Spanish government for sinking the vessel. The national anger convinced President McKinley that he must provide the leadership to resolve the festering Cuban imbroglio before the emotions stemming from it disrupted American society. [2]

Late in March the chief executive issued a series of demands to Spain, which in his judgment represented the minimum action that the people of the United States would accept as a resolution to the impasse on the Caribbean island. When the Madrid government refused to accede fully to them, McKinley on 11 April asked Congress for authority to use the army and the navy to end hostilities. That body responded on 19 April by declaring Cuba to be a free and independent nation. The legislators empowered the president to use United States armed forces to liberate the new country if Spain did not vacate it voluntarily. [3]

Americans were united in their determination to rescue the Cubans from Spanish tyranny, and they did not intend to profit from this assumption of responsibility. The Senate and the House of Representatives attached an amendment to the declaration of war that disclaimed any intention on the part of the United States of annexing the island. After voting for action against Spain, members of Congress gathered outside their chambers jovially singing ditties improvised for the occasion. One dedicated to the Spanish army commander in Cuba contained the line, "We'll Hang General Weyler to a Sour Apple Tree." The musical solons also alternated between Union and Confederate songs, such as "The Battle Hymn of the Republic" and "Dixie." During the ensuing hostili-

ties Americans made much of the fact that a generation after Appomattox the veterans of the blue and the grey, or their sons, were fighting side by side. The Spanish-American War proved to be a conflict of short duration. Secretary of State John Hay dubbed it "a splendid little war," but it hardly seemed that to the Light Guardsmen and their comrades who served in that often deadly struggle. [4]

The United States in the years after the Civil War had maintained a modern navy as its first line of defense. National leaders felt that the country could rapidly and effectively raise a large land force in case of war by supplementing a rather small standing army with volunteers from state troops whose militia training would have given them the fundamentals of professionalism even if they were not full-time soldiers. One senator of the 1890s expressed a popular sentiment of the day when he said that "an army could be raised in a day, and drilled and disciplined in thirty days." If such statements were a trifle optimistic, nevertheless they contained basic assumptions about the late-nineteenth-century militia as it was blending into the form that would eventually become the modern National Guard. By the early 1890s the term "National Guard" had come to replace that of "militia" in Michigan, as it had in virtually every other state in this country. Michigan officially adopted the new wording in 1893. [5]

Indeed, in an incredibly short period of time the United States Army would have to expand to a much larger size for its conflict with Spain. Even before the president had called for state troops, Governor Hazen Pingree issued a formal summons for the Michigan National Guard to assemble at Camp Eaton at Island Lake within seventy-two hours. Already in session in early April 1898, the legislature had passed a number of key laws to facilitate Michigan's wartime effort. These measures included the authorization of the sale of five hundred thousand dollars worth of war bonds to aid in the preparation of the state's militia for any necessary national service. "The governor is tickled," reported a local newspaper, "over the military bill that was passed by the senate and house."[6]

On 23 April the president issued his formal call for state forces. Under procedures established by the War Department, each state governor would pick an appropriate location at which that commonwealth's soldiers would assemble and receive medical examinations. Those deemed in good health would then be given the opportunity to volunteer for the army of the United States. In 1898 popular support for the war was so substantial that federal authorities had a greater fear that men not physically fit would try to enter the service than concern that able-bodied men would shirk their duty toward their country.[7]

On the eve of the conflict with Spain, both the Detroit Light Guard and its dissident offshoot, the Detroit Light Infantry, were battalions in the Fourth Michigan, a regiment with a particularly distinguished record. The two militia units might have entered a period of rapprochement, but the potential friendliness had been disrupted by a series of disputes which continued as late as January 1898 over the election in 1894 of a colonel for the regiment. The Light Infantry's resentment might well have been exacerbated by the feeling that it was being overshadowed in the Fourth Michigan by the greater age, prestige, and influence of the Light Guard.[8]

This squabbling convinced Governor Pingree and his advisers on the State Military Board that the Fourth Michigan could not continue with its existing organization, and in March 1898 they issued orders to dissolve the regiment and divide it into two independent battalions. By an administrative quirk the younger of the groups, the Light Infantry, was established as the First Battalion, which also included the other Detroit militia groups, the Scott Guards and the Montgomery Rifles. Eventually these were affiliated with the Second Infantry, later the Thirty-second Infantry, which consisted mostly of Grand Rapids units.[9]

The Light Guard became the Second Independent Battalion. Captain Charles W. Harrah of Company A of the unit was appointed acting major of this battalion and was soon formally elected to that post. The Light Guard would on 6 May become part of a reorganized First Infantry, which within a week became the Thirty-first Infantry, because Governor Pingree insisted that the Michigan regiments in 1898 take up their numbering where the state units in the Civil War had ended, to avoid any confusion in official records as well as to provide historical continuity.[10]

As the troops began to arrive at Camp Eaton for training, state officials made it clear that appropriate behavior, including abstemious personal habits, would be expected of the men. Adjutant General Edwin Irish created a provost guard of twenty-nine men "to preserve peace and to arrest every soldier who misbehaves." In speaking to a special assembly of potential soldiers, Irish assured them that Michigan was proud of its recruits but that a tiny handful of rowdies had embarrassed their comrades by unacceptable, disruptive behavior. Such offenders, the adjutant general warned, were laboring under the assumption that they had gathered together at Island Lake to have a good time rather than to prepare to meet a national crisis. "I shall have no objection to any here who wish to get drunk," indicated Irish, meaning that any inebriated soldier would simply be placed on the next train out. "For every drunkard there are one hundred respectable young men in Michigan anxious for their places [sic]."[11]

From the first the men at Camp Eaton were subject to a particularly rigorous professional regime. The basics of drilling were reviewed, and especially demanding exercises were carried out to give the troops practice in living under actual field conditions. The entire process was designed so that the citizen-soldiers would undergo a proper toughening in order that they would easily blend into the regular army and be receptive to the even more advanced training they would receive in the federal forces.[12]

A number of the state's best physicians made up the corps of specialists who gave the necessary physical examinations. The process involved much difficulty. Not only was the number of medical officers modest compared to the large group of men to be inspected, but also most recruits were so eager to serve in the war that they concealed deficiencies rather than be rejected. Many of the individuals, however, proved to be in inadequate physical shape for national service, a commentary on the general state of health in the United States in the 1890s. Many of the ailments of the approximately 20 percent who failed to meet the standards seemed to derive from smoking. "You who are suffering from 'smoker's heart,'" commented one officer, "would do well to stop smoking a few days before physical examination."[13]

Men who did not meet the medical criteria were colloquially referred to as "plucked," and many of them tried again and sometimes managed through bluff and persistence to pass the requirements. On the other hand, those who were unable despite all efforts to meet the health standards were dismayed. One rejected youth moaned, "It's the biggest disappointment I ever experienced in my life." Many young men had given up well-paying jobs for the chance to risk their lives serving their country for thirteen dollars a month. They were so disconsolate when they realized they would not be able to go to war that "some linger[ed] around, hoping to have their cases reconsidered, but once 'plucked' they [were] done for." On 8 May 1898 the briefly designated First Michigan, including most companies of the Detroit Light Guard, was mustered into the service of the United States in front of an enthusiastic crowd that had assembled at Camp Eaton to witness the event.[14]

The Wolverine soldiers were eager to depart for federal army camp for advanced training, but, among a multitude of other factors, a shortage of equipment delayed them. Hazen Pingree and other Michigan leaders extended themselves to provide their volunteers with the necessary accoutrements of war, even though the ultimate responsibility for outfitting them rested with the national authorities. However, as Adjutant General Irish commented, "Anyone who has studied the civil war must know that unless each state fits out their troops they will begin to die off before the government can issue them supplies."[15]

In mid-May the newly named Thirty-first Michigan headed for Camp Thomas at Chickamauga, Tennessee, while its brothers of the Light Infantry went to Tampa, Florida, with the Thirty-second. One company of the Light Guard, however, was attached to a third regiment, and ironically this body became the only segment of Detroit's oldest militia group to see actual service in Cuba during the Spanish-American War.[16]

The Light Guard served as an independent volunteer militia group as well as a unit in the Michigan National Guard. "The members of the Detroit Light Guard play a dual roll; in one they are amenable only to the state, and in the other to the Light Guard organization," one commentator observed. The unit also absorbed smaller and newer militias into its ranks in the generation after the Civil War. One such group, originally the St. John's Cadets, officially became part of the Detroit Light Guard in January 1896 as Company M. The legislature had specified that "the state troops shall be composed of not exceeding forty companies of infantry, beyond which in time of peace there shall be no increase." The result of this policy was that a company of volunteer militia might be active but unable to join the state's National Guard until a vacancy developed among the maximum number of units permitted in the Michigan military establishment. Thus, Company M was still on the waiting list for the Michigan National Guard when the Spanish-American War began.[17]

An opening in the Michigan Guard would occur when an existing company was deactivated or dropped out. If a place did not become available,

the leaders of the Light Guard hoped that the law would be changed to expand the number of units permitted in the state troops. When Governor Pingree issued the call for the Wolverine State's military forces to assemble at Island Lake, Company M still had not been integrated into the Michigan National Guard; consequently, the former did not leave with the rest of the battalion. Determined to join their brothers, the men and officers of the temporarily orphaned unit decided to accept a vacancy that appeared in the Thirty-third Michigan Infantry, and they departed for Island Lake from the Light Guard Armory on 15 May. Although they left Detroit much later than their comrades had, they received a warm send-off from well-wishers, including Mayor Maybury and cheering members of the Veteran Corps.[18]

Upon reaching Island Lake, Company M was quickly mustered into its new unit, becoming part of the volunteer force of the United States Army. Since the Thirty-first and Thirty-second Regiments had already left for training camps in the South, the members of the Thirty-third felt great eagerness to move in that direction. The Michigan congressional delegation urged the secretary of war, Russell A. Alger, a native of its state, to send this group to Camp Alger near the nation's capital. Apparently the Wolverine solons felt that since the other two units were stationed at Chickamauga and Tampa, having an additional regiment at another location might maximize the chance for the state's troops to see action in the campaign to liberate Cuba. When the Thirty-third Regiment arrived in camp on 30 May, Secretary Alger took much trouble to look after its needs, even though he was overwhelmed with the endless details of military mobilization and numerous other problems, including a false rumor that a Spanish fleet had just been seen off the coast of New York.[19]

While at Camp Alger the men of Company M delighted in the news that Light Guard Colonel Henry M. Duffield had just been appointed a brigadier general and that his brigade would include the Thirty-third and Thirty-fourth Michigan Regiments together with the Ninth Massachusetts. During their stay in the Potomac area, Colonel Boynton and the senior officers of the Thirty-third received the singular honor of a visit to the Capitol and the White House under the sponsorship of the Michigan congressional delegation. President McKinley commented, "I shall expect great things from the Thirty-third Michigan when they get into action."[20]

The stay at Camp Alger was short and intensive. The Wolverines received final and thorough training for actual battle conditions in the tropics, which were often extremely difficult and unpleasant. Yet when a solicitous home-state congressman came out from Washington to see if the men were comfortable, one Light Guard officer replied, "We are soldiers, and did not come here to kick, but to obey orders."[21]

The soldiers were eager for combat, but before they could be sent the McKinley administration had to make a number of key strategic and tactical decisions. In particular, the secretary of war and the commanding officer of the United States Army, Major General Nelson A. Miles, an irascible Civil War veteran, had to work out a plan that met with the president's approval. The federal leaders selected Tampa as the principal staging area at which the Fifth Army Corps would assemble for

an invasion of Cuba. But other ports would also figure in the operation, and, thus, the Thirty-third Michigan embarked from Newport News, Virginia.[22]

General Miles had wanted to delay the attack on the island until late in the fall to avoid the unfavorable battle conditions caused by the summer rainy season. President McKinley, however, wished to launch military operations at once because he felt "that [it] would help force the quickest possible victory" and save American lives. Figuring also in the chief executive's decision was the fact that the Spanish naval commander Admiral Cervera and his "forlorn squadron" had taken refuge at Santiago de Cuba, where they were hemmed in by United States maritime forces. The president ordered an immediate invasion by the Fifth Army. He anticipated that a successful assault on Santiago would result in the capture of not only a major enemy citadel and garrison but the opposition fleet as well.[23]

Meanwhile at Camp Alger the men of General Duffield's brigade continued to train in an atmosphere charged with rumors, hopes, and anxieties about the possibility of their going into action. On 20 June after having returned from an especially arduous march, the members of the Michigan Thirty-third and Thirty-fourth enthusiastically received the news that they would soon be embarking for Cuba to rendezvous with the Fifth Army Corps, which was commanded by yet another Wolverine, General William Shafter. As a young man he had served with great distinction in the Civil War and afterwards remained in the regular army. His seniority and perseverance earned him the rank of major general at the outbreak of the Spanish-American War. Because of Shafter's great bulk (he weighed more than three hundred pounds), some who served with him liked to quip that their commander was a "floating tent."[24]

Duffield's brigade was transported by a combination of railroad and "bay steamer" to Fortress Monroe, Virginia. It then boarded the SS *Yale* at Newport News and set sail for Caribbean waters. After an uneventful voyage remembered by some only for the monotony of a diet that consisted of "canned tomatoes, and canned beef, . . . with hard tack and coffee," they reached the coast near Santiago on 26 June. The main body of the Fifth Army had arrived almost a week before.[25]

Santiago de Cuba had a garrison of ten thousand men. Although the civilian and military populations had suffered greatly from the American naval blockade, the town was defended by well-trained, well-entrenched troops. Many of the United States soldiers, on the other hand, were untested in actual combat. The men of Company M and their comrades were soon jumping into "the cutters and whale boats" that would carry them from the *Yale* to the beach. The smaller craft "were coupled together in trains of four or five, towed by steam launches from the navy." The men "found it was no easy matter to get ashore through the surf, each weighted down with a hundred rounds of ammunition." Fortified heights on the ocean side made the town extremely difficult to attack. Shafter consequently decided to risk an overland march to fall upon the area from the rear.[26]

This plan to avoid the casualties inherent in a frontal assault involved dangers of its own. Shafter realized this because he had studied the history of an eighteenth-century British army that had attempted the same back-door invasion route. This journey through "yellow-fever country" had so debilitated the Englishmen that they were in no condition to fight as they neared their goal and had to withdraw. With this lesson in mind, the portly commander knew "that the sole chance of success would lie in the very impetuosity of his attack," for he would have to "seek a quick decision before disease defeated him."[27]

Shafter, therefore, moved swiftly to position his expeditionary force to the east of Santiago. Duffield's brigade was stationed at Siboney and had the responsibility of making a feint to detain Spanish troops in the vicinity of Aguadores, a nearby point. The scene of action was near the coast, and the Michiganians were to be supported by a naval bombardment. The center of the attack involved the Aguadores Bridge, where the Spanish had effective fortifications. Consequently, the latter were not substantially affected by the shelling from the United States ships. As the men of Company M and their comrades went out to battle on the morning of 1 July, they began a grueling expedition. They moved through the most difficult kind of terrain, for "the denseness of a Cuban jungle can be appreciated only by one who attempts to penetrate it. Every bush that grows in it bears a thorn."[28]

The troops were also uncomfortably burdened by a load of equipment that typically included "a carbine, a hundred rounds of ammunition, canteen, poncho, half a shelter tent, the army blanket, rations and other necessary articles." The uniforms in which the Michiganians had to fight, moreover, seemed to have been better designed for Alaska than Cuba. A particular problem for the American troops in this area stemmed from the lack of availability of up-to-date equipment. Most of them lacked the especially desirable Krag-Jörgensen rifle. In the words of the brigade commander, "Our troops, who were at great disadvantage because of their Springfield rifles and smoky powder, at once discovered their location to the enemy, while the latter were armed with Mausers and smokeless powder."[29]

General Duffield's assignment involved expending a minimal number of his men to divert the attention of the enemy troops in the Aguadores area so they would not send aid to the main body of defenders of Santiago. A deep ravine, flooded by the rapidly flowing San Juan River, which was especially treacherous during the rainy season, separated the United States forces from their foes. About one hundred feet of the bridge across the stream had been blown up and the rest, the Americans correctly suspected, had been mined. Although General Duffield lacked boats, he positioned his men in such a skillful manner that the Spanish commander expected an all-out assault rather then a feint. Thus, the men of Company M and the others of the Thirty-third Michigan kept the enemy off-balance and afraid to abandon their defensive positions.[30]

Confronted with a river that could not be crossed, Duffield declined a quixotic young officer's offer to attempt to swim it to reconnoiter. Instead the brigadier general instructed "Col. Boynton to send forward a line of skirmishers, supporting them with a battalion. . . . The remainder of the regiment was put in position in the woods on each side of the track." In spite of the backing of concerted naval fire, in taking their places Company M's companions in L unit suffered five casualties, two of

them fatal. The Thirty-third did have sharpshooters in an advanced post. Their task was to keep the foe off-balance by maintaining an effective fire, but their old-fashioned smoke-producing rifles put them at a disadvantage with the Spanish.[31]

About three o'clock in the afternoon of 1 July Duffield's men began to regroup for withdrawal. The Americans safely moved back to Siboney by train. Despite their exhaustion and sadness over the casualties of the whole unit, six wounded and two killed, the members of the Thirty-third Michigan Volunteer Infantry were exuberant over their first successful experience in combat.[32]

These events, however, had not completed the work of the regiment. General Shafter, pleased with the accomplishments of Duffield's brigade in its first action, ordered it to continue the diversion the next day. Once again the Michiganians tested their fighting mettle in the tropical heat. Major Webb's Third Battalion, including Company M, took its position in a strategic and dangerous area. Despite all precautions, it was in an exposed location if the enemy decided to mount a powerful offensive in its direction. The success of the main United States attack on the Spanish fortifications on the heights of San Juan on 1 July and the follow-up actions on the second and third, however, protected the Americans at Aguadores as well as eliminating the need for further campaigning there.[33]

Companies I and L returned at once to Siboney after the victory at San Juan Heights, while Companies M and K retired to a more defensible position than the advanced post they had been occupying. They protected their new location with trenches that they playfully named Camp Webb.

There the Light Guardsmen and their comrades continued under much stress, since "the men of both companies were required to remain awake during the night, and both companies alternately took twenty-four hours charge of the outpost work. On the outposts, every man able to muster was made use of and posted in pairs, relieving each other every six hours."[34]

Meanwhile, on 3 July, a hot and clear Sunday, Admiral Cervera prepared to escape from the city's harbor with his squadron as the Spanish military position at Santiago crumbled. Action began at 9:35 A.M., when the *Infanta María Teresa*, at the head of the fleet, tried to sally forth through the narrow opening left in the channel by the sunken vessels placed there by the blockading United States Navy. The attempt to escape failed; American ships sank or drove ashore all the enemy ships by early afternoon. An exuberant Admiral Sampson reported to President McKinley that his forces offered "the nation as a Fourth of July present the whole of Cervera's fleet."[35]

This naval engagement, coming in the wake of the overwhelming American success on land, meant that at the end of the first three days in July all possibility of effective resistance at Santiago de Cuba had ended, although the Spanish still controlled the town itself. Shafter rejected importunate advice that he storm the town. Although his forces were strong enough to seize the citadel, the general felt the resulting loss of life could not be justified under the circumstances. The beleaguered Spanish troops as well as the civilian population were existing on such limited rations, largely consisting of rice, that they could not hold out for long. Indeed on 15 July, General José Toral, commander of the garrison, agreed to surrender. The actual ceremony took place on the morning of the seventeenth, Secretary Alger reported, "and at noon our entire army lined up along the trenches, and greeted with cheers the raising of the Stars and Stripes on the Governor's Palace. . . . A salute of twenty-one guns was fired, and our bands played the 'Star Spangled Banner.'"[36]

When the news reached the men of Company M, their joy at the victory was intensified by the prospect of being able to leave their particularly distressing field conditions. The Michiganians had been ensconced at "Camp Webb" with minimal shelter during a period in which tropical rains alternated with fierce, unrelenting sun and attendant heat. So it was with the greatest delight that the men relinquished their exposed and uncomfortable outpost and rejoined the main regiment at Siboney. In their enthusiasm upon returning from a trying, exhausting experience, they used the ocean for bathing.[37]

Even though the principal fighting in Cuba had ceased and the men of Company M had joined their brigade, the hardships had not ended. Although an improvement over "Camp Webb," Siboney hardly constituted a tropical resort. Indeed, it was a pesthole. Yellow fever broke out among the troops, with thirty-six cases among the Wolverines alone. General Duffield also became ill with it. Soon, malaria and dysentery began to decimate the ranks. One writer observes that "disease wrecked the Fifth Corps at Santiago almost before General Shafter could consolidate his victory over the Spaniards."[38]

After their defeat at Santiago, enemy forces still held out in western Cuba; the United

States leadership, however, decided that subsequent campaigning should focus on Puerto Rico, which contained the last important stronghold of Spanish strength in the Caribbean. Although a key role had been envisioned for the Fifth Army Corps in any such action, the deteriorating health of that group rendered it incapable of performing such a task.[39] Illness became so rampant that the corps's commander "suspended the customary rifle volleys and bugle calls at burials lest their frequency undermine morale. . . . Shafter's troops degenerated into a mob of shambling scarecrows." For the Light Guardsmen of Company M the quality of life became particularly spartan after General Miles arrived at Siboney and, at the urging of medical experts, ordered the entire hamlet razed. A camp song represented the feelings of the Michiganians as they were busy burning buildings that harbored germs:

> Snakes as long as Halstead Streat,
> Flies and skeeters that can't be beat.
> Oh, how we want to leave Cuba,
> Lord, how we want to go home![40]

The War Department had originally been reluctant to allow the Fifth Army Corps to return home, if only until the yellow fever had run its course among its members. By late July, however, the federal government had secured a tract of land on Long Island to use as a site for a "rest and recuperation camp" for the veterans who had served in Cuba. Meanwhile, the glacial pace of withdrawing the United States troops created a sense of despair in Shafter's command, and he called a "council of his general officers and chief surgeons" to discuss the situation. The conference resulted in a letter signed by key members of the general's staff which urged that their men be brought home as rapidly as possible. When this communication, labeled a "Round Robin," splashed across the nation's press on 4 August it created something of a sensation.[41]

The ensuing uproar may have hastened the movement of the ailing heroes of Santiago towards home. By 7 August the decision had been made to transfer the Thirty-third Michigan to Montauk Point, Long Island. Prior to embarkation the Michiganians, following instructions, stripped and took vigorous baths in the ocean, emerging to find their old clothing burned and replaced with clean underwear and new, lighter uniforms. The swim, more comfortable dress, and the prospect of returning home served as a strong tonic to the flagging spirits of the Wolverines. The men who had arrived in Cuba aboard the transport *Yale* were assigned to a sister ship, the *Harvard,* for the voyage back.[42]

The small vessel, called a lighter, which was to convey the men from the shore to the troop ship, struck an obstacle, and the men of the Thirty-third suddenly found themselves struggling in the offshore waters. Luckily no loss of life occurred because of their efficient rescue by other small craft, but a considerable amount of luggage was never recovered. The soldiers had to spend the night without shelter. The next morning transportation became available that finally conveyed them successfully to their ship.[43]

As they steamed out of the harbor at Santiago, the members of the Thirty-third Michigan felt justifiable pride in the part they had played in achieving the United States victory there. While they exuberantly hailed the Stars and Stripes flying from the captured Spanish citadel of the Morro Castle, they could reflect with satisfaction on the manner in which they conducted themselves in their test in combat. The men of Company M and their comrades in Duffield's brigade had served with distinction and bravery under grueling and perilous conditions. Tropical disease had decimated their ranks more than the enemy's bullets had.[44]

The *Harvard* substantially retraced the route that the *Yale* had followed in bringing the Thirty-third to Cuba in June. The voyage was marred by the death of one soldier, who had to be buried at sea. Otherwise, the journey to Long Island took place without incident. Just as Secretary Alger had personally wished farewell to the departing troops from his state two months earlier, he was on hand to welcome them when the transport docked. While the band played "Michigan, My Michigan," the secretary of war personally shook hands with each Wolverine veteran as he stepped ashore.[45]

Once the men reached Montauk Point, they were quartered at Camp Wikoff, named after the highest-ranking American officer killed in Cuba. President McKinley, along with Russell Alger, visited the soldiers while they were in New York, and the two dignitaries did not hesitate to go into the wards filled with those ill with infectious fevers, a brave act in an age when medical knowledge could accomplish only modest feats in treating the ailments. Governor Hazen Pingree, who keenly remembered his days in combat and as a prisoner of the Confederates during the Civil War, sent a delegation to represent the state's concern for its veterans. The party included nurses, Colonel George

A. Loud of the State Military Board, and one of Pingree's own sons.[46]

On 2 September 1898 the Thirty-third and Thirty-fourth Michigan Regiments started for home by rail. The journey was such a slow and difficult one that at times it must have seemed an extension of the Cuban campaigning to the weary and recuperating soldiers. "The train was sent around most of the cities, on the through freight cut-offs, and this switching kept [the troops] from much abundant refreshment hastily prepared by public spirited people in the places ahead." The officers and the sick had sleepers, but the late summer heat created uncomfortable conditions in all the cars as well as giving the Wolverines an unpleasant reminder of the tropical Cuban heat. Even the continual fare of coffee and sandwiches prompted the men to recall the monotony of rations in the field.[47]

The War Department had planned to have all of the Michigan regiments of General Duffield's brigade report to Camp Eaton at Island Lake, the camp from which they had originally departed. Pingree, however, used his influence to have the two combat units sent directly to Detroit so that they might receive an appropriately warm reception there. The crowd at the railroad station was one of the most enthusiastic assemblies ever to gather at the city on the straits. The train was scheduled to arrive at the inconvenient hour of 1:00 A.M. Nevertheless, by midnight a massive number of Detroiters had turned out with unbridled enthusiasm to greet the returning warriors. Members of the Naval Reserves as well as the city police force had been mobilized to aid in crowd control. Public officials felt that the volume of well-wishers would be so enormous that good intentions might accidentally convert a joyous event into tragedy unless the jubilant spirits were held in check by careful and tactful management. Indeed, as the good-natured citizens swarmed through the streets, the ambulances, carriages, and delivery wagons assembled for use on this occasion added to the congestion.[48]

As the train bearing the veterans of the Santiago campaign chugged into the station, the returning men of Company M were greeted by the Light Guard Band playing "Home, Sweet Home" and the applause of spectators. The detraining soldiers of Detroit's oldest militia were then escorted to the armory by its Veteran Corps. During the march members of the Light Infantry voluntarily fell into step. This gracious gesture marked the beginning of a final healing of the unfortunate split between the two groups and anticipated the dissidents' rejoining the parent organization within a few years.[49]

At the Light Guard Armory, despite the late hour, an emotional reunion took place between the returning soldiers and their families and friends. The Detroiters were especially delighted to learn that no member of Company M had been killed during the campaign, although some were still absent because they were recovering from wounds or service-related illnesses. The hour of the ceremony precluded much of the ponderous oratory so common to the period. Mayor Maybury, however, could not resist expressing some words of appreciation to the group of volunteers who had represented the city in the actual fighting in Cuba during the Spanish-American War.[50]

When Company M had gone from Island Lake to Camp Alger to service in the Santiago campaign, the other three companies from Detroit had continued to participate in the volunteer army, although to their extreme distress they were unable to take part directly in the fray. Their experience, however, paralleled that of the vast majority of those who joined the American armed services during the war of 1898. Those individuals who flocked into the country's military forces but did not actually reach the battlefield, however, played a significant role in the rapid achievement of success: for the very size of the army the United States was quickly able to amass, along with the victories in the combat zones, led to the Spanish decision to sue for peace in August 1898.

These three companies of the Light Guard, A, B, and F, changed to I, K, and L respectively, left Island Lake for Camp Thomas, named for one of the Union heroes of the Civil War and situated at Chickamauga, Tennessee. This location had the advantage of acclimatizing the Michiganians to temperatures roughly halfway between those of the Wolverine State and Cuba. The members of the Light Guard assiduously prepared themselves, under Spartan conditions, for a campaign in which they would not serve. The men of the Thirty-first, of which Companies I, K, and L were part, did achieve the enviable reputation of belonging to one of the best drilled among the volunteer regiments, earning plaudits from out-of-state observers as well as those from their home. Governor Hazen Pingree himself came to observe the polished Wolverine troops. A high level of discipline was maintained among the men. At other locations the tedium of training camp without the opportunity to leave for combat sometimes led to excessive drinking. The moonshine available to volunteers "became known as 'two-step,' because after drinking it no one could take more than two steps without falling over." The Light Guardsmen and their regimental colleagues, however, retained good military order unmarred by "one good case of square drunk."[51]

The grinding routine of preparing for battlefield duty that did not come to pass would from time to time be enlivened by rumors that the Michiganians were about to be dispatched to Tampa as a staging area for an allegedly impending Puerto Rican campaign. Such expectations failed to materialize. Some of the Light Guardsmen became so anxious for active service that when another unit left for the port of Newport News "nine members of the Light Guard companies took 'French leave' and attempted to go with it, but a detail, posted after them with hot haste, spoiled the game. The guardhouse yawned for them, and a heavy fine swallowed most of their pay."[52]

As the men of the Thirty-first despaired of their chance to avenge the destruction of the *Maine*, a story circulated in the ranks of the unit that it should be named the "Chickamauga Park Improvement Association." The recruits dealt with their frustrations by joking about them; and often employed rather heavy-handed ethnic humor. One such jest was "A stranger approached a guard and asked, 'Are you a sentinel, sir?' The soldier responded: 'No, I am a Swede.'"[53]

The volunteers who never left the United States for service abroad, however, were not immune from danger. Many of the training camps were pestholes of disease, and the Thirty-first found itself in a place riddled with illness at Camp Thomas. Perhaps for reasons of health the regiment moved its campsite almost two miles away from its original location early in August 1898. Since the war was obviously winding down without the Michiganians going overseas, they erected near their tents a mock "tombstone, bearing the inscription, 'No hope for the 31st. August 4th, 1898,' and surmounted it with a wreath of red handkerchiefs." This article of apparel comprised a characteristic part of the unit's uniform.[54]

These pessimistic expectations proved to be correct, for on 12 August 1898 the Spanish government agreed to an armistice bringing an end to the fighting. A need, nevertheless, continued for troops both to bolster the nation's defenses until the final peace treaty was signed and to maintain garrisons in the recently liberated and unstable areas of Cuba and the Philippines. With the cessation of hostilities, however, the enthusiasm for the war rapidly diminished at Camp Thomas. Moreover, concern about the unhealthy conditions at that location resulted in the War Department's ordering the Thirty-first Michigan to move in mid-August to Camp Poland near Knoxville, Tennessee. There the bracing air of the Great Smoky Mountains was regarded as more salubrious for the Michiganians. Sentiment grew among the Wolverines in favor of a return to civilian life since chances for participation in active campaigns had vanished.[55]

This feeling must have intensified by New Year's Day 1899, when the soldiers from Michigan found themselves the last unit at Camp Poland. In the midst of snow that swept down on the Tennessee mountains, many members of the group still dreamed of a tour of duty in the tropics. These hopefuls consequently were delighted to learn in the first week of January that their regiment had just received orders to leave for Savannah, Georgia, preparatory to embarking for Cuba to serve with the army of occupation there. The stay in that Georgia town proved an exceedingly pleasant although short one as the Michiganians developed an extremely amicable relationship with the militiamen from the Peach State. Late in the month the Thirty-first departed for the Caribbean on the transport *Chester*. [56]

Arriving on the Cuban coast on 1 February, the unit landed the next morning. An advanced expedition at once departed by train for Rodrigo, "a station about sixty miles north of Cienfuegos, for the purpose of preparing camp for the regiment." Several days later the Light Guard Battalion entrained for this new post. The men made the three-hour journey in uncomfortable boxcars. Once they had arrived they pitched tents and settled down to the routine of their duties in a poverty-stricken rural area. The Michiganians, like so many other United States troops who had volunteered in 1898, felt they were fighting for the liberation of oppressed islanders whom the soldiers identified with the American colonists of 1776. The midwesterners, consequently, were often surprised and even dismayed to encounter people of a background that seemed so alien to them. The Light Guardsmen, nevertheless, extended themselves to try to understand the local inhabitants. Baseball sometimes served as a bridge of communication that crossed cultures. An intramural game among the soldiers attracted an interested audience of local inhabitants. The troops even played some informal matches with local teams. On another occasion the Light Guardsmen, comprehending the universal importance of a solemn ceremony,

punctiliously attended funeral services for a Cuban officer who had led the rebels in that vicinity. [57]

The duties of the Detroit battalion could sometimes involve action as intriguing as appearing at the town of Caibarien to protect from possible bandits the considerable payroll funds that had been amassed there on one occasion. In most instances, however, the Michiganians found themselves confined to the grinding monotony of garrison life. Even if not dramatic, the services of the Thirty-first played a vital role in maintaining the stability of Cuban society during the difficult and delicate transition that the Caribbean nation was making to an independent republic. The troops, nevertheless, were not sorry when they learned after a short period of time that their tour of duty as an army of occupation was coming to an end and that they would be boarding the transport *Thomas* for a return home by the second week in April. They had been happy to serve their country overseas, although disappointed not to have been able to take part in the fighting. They were pleased, though, to complete their obligation before the island's unhealthy rainy season had set in. [58]

A little more than a year after they had left for Island Lake, the members of the Light Guard Battalion returned to Detroit for a rousing reception, with Governor Pingree and Mayor Maybury leading the festivities. As the returning veterans marched from the train station to the armory, they passed the Cadillac Hotel where a steamboat whistle had been set up and was "going at full blast . . . booming a noisy note of welcome until long after the parade had passed." As the unit proceeded past the city hall, "'WELCOME OUR BOYS' flashed out in brilliant electric letters in red and white and blue." Once they reached their destination the reception became even more tumultuous and enthusiastic. After a fortunately limited diet of late-nineteenth-century oratory, the men were able to turn to a more pleasing menu. General Duffield, demonstrating his usual leadership, gave the shortest and most popular speech of the evening, "Eat," and those assembled obeyed him.[59]

Notes

1. E. May, 78, 113, 117; Jack C. Dierks, *A Leap to Arms: The Cuban Campaign of 1898* (Philadelphia, 1970), 14; Graham A. Cosmas, *An Army for Empire: The United States Army in the Spanish-American War* (Columbia, Mo., 1971), 19–20.

2. E. May, 136–43; Dierks, 19–21.

3. E. May, 152–59; Dierks, 23–24; David F. Trask, *The War with Spain in 1898* (New York, 1981), 39–56.

4. Dierks, 24; R. A. Alger, *The Spanish-American War* (New York, 1901), 6; E. May, 220.

5. Clowes, 91–92, 99; Mahon, 110; *Compiled Laws of the State of Michigan* (1897), vol. 1, title 2, pt. 8, chap. 2, sec. 6: 571. Statute adopted 1 June 1893; effective 28 Aug. 1893.

6. Henry M. Utley, *Michigan as a State, from the Close of the Civil War to the End of the Nineteenth Century*, vol. 4 of Utley and Byron M. Cutcheon, *Michigan as a Province, Territory and State, the Twenty-Sixth Member of the Federal Union* (New York, 1906), 241; Clowes, 106; *Detroit Free Press*, 17 Apr. 1898; *Detroit Evening News*, 15 Apr. 1898.

7. Alger, 18, 21; *Detroit Tribune*, 8 May 1898.

8. Clowes, 85–89.

9. Ibid., 88–89; *Detroit Evening News*, 25 Mar. 1898; *Detroit Tribune*, 26 Mar., 8 May 1898; *Detroit Free Press*, 9, 14 May 1898.

10. Utley, 242; *Detroit Free Press*, 7, 10, 11, 13, 15 May 1898; Clowes, 122–27.

11. *Detroit Free Press*, 29 Apr. 1898.

12. Clowes, 112–14.

13. *Detroit Free Press*, 5, 7, 8 May 1898.

14. *Detroit Free Press*, 8, 9, 11, 13 May 1898.

15. *Detroit Free Press*, 10 May 1898.

16. Clowes, 108, 156; *Detroit Free Press*, 15–23 May, 1898.

17. Clowes, 78–80; *Compiled Laws of the State of Michigan* (1897), vol. 1, title 2, pt. 8, chap. 2, sec. 7: 572.

18. Clowes, 79–80, 137–41; *Detroit Free Press*, 17 May 1898.

19. Clowes, 141, 145–46; Alger, 21, 29–30, 37–40.

20. Clowes, 145–49.

21. Ibid., 145–47.

22. Trask, 146, 166–69, 215; Clowes, 155–56.

23. Trask, 168–75.

24. Clowes, 155–56; Trask, 180; G. J. A. O'Toole, *The Spanish War, An American Epic—1898* (New York, 1984), 255.

25. Clowes, 157–59; Trask, 194.

26. Clowes, 160; Trask, 198–208.

27. Trask, 206.

28. Clowes, 160–63; Trask, 213–17; Alger, 121.

29. Trask, 217; Dierks, 97–98; Cosmas, 202, 212; Alger, 108; Clowes, 163.

30. Clowes, 162–65; Alger, 128–30; O'Toole, 295; Trask, 225–26.

31. Clowes, 163.

32. Ibid., 165.

33. Ibid., 165–70; Trask, 244–47.

34. Clowes, 167–68.

35. Trask, 261–66.

36. Alger, 216–20; Trask, 286–319.

37. Clowes, 172–75.

38. Ibid., 172–74; Cosmas, 230, 251.

39. Trask, 324–25; Cosmas, 251–57.

40. Cosmas, 252; Clowes, 172–73; Trask, 327.

41. Cosmas, 256–58; Alger, 256–73.

42. Clowes, 177–78; Cosmas, 258–59.

43. Clowes, 178–79.

44. Ibid., 179.

45. Ibid., 180–81.

46. Ibid., 181–82.

47. Ibid., 183–85.

48. Ibid., 186.

49. Ibid., 187–88.

50. Ibid., 188–89.

51. Ibid., 126, 130, 212–13; Trask, 191.

52. Clowes, 229–32.

53. Ibid., 231; Trask, 191.

54. Trask, 160; Clowes, 234.

55. Clowes, 237–42.

56. Ibid., 272–77.

57. Ibid., 281–87.

58. Ibid., 285–305.

59. Ibid., 326–30.

World War I

The history of Detroit and its Light Guard becomes more intricately bound with the history of the United States and the world in the twentieth century. Rapidly changing technology continued to make the globe a smaller and more precarious place in which to live. In the first years of the 1900s, however, it seemed as if the services of the Light Guard would be required primarily to help maintain domestic tranquility. During July 1913 the Detroit militiamen were dispatched to the Upper Peninsula to preserve order in a copper strike during a period in which labor disputes in the United States were especially susceptible to violence. Whatever the distressing aspects of having to keep peace in a situation having many characteristics of a bitter family quarrel, the Light Guard soon would be involved in major challenges that made the events of 1913 seem minor by comparison.[1]

In 1914 the Great War, as the First World War was often called, erupted in Europe. This situation abroad perhaps gave added urgency to the emphasis all units of the Michigan National Guard placed in that period to devoting their energies to training, in particular in their annual encampment at the "new Military Reservation at Grayling, Michigan." Preparation, though, was soon interrupted by a conflict closer to home.[2]

Early in the 1900s Mexico was swept by revolution, which left that nation in a state of turmoil. President Woodrow Wilson had begun his first administration in 1913 by pledging a more idealistic approach to the affairs of Latin America than his predecessors had exhibited in such doctrines as "Dollar Diplomacy." The complex realities of Mexican politics, however, led Wilson to become enmeshed in that nation's internal affairs. By 1916 the regime that had emerged out of the maelstrom of revolutionary politics was that of President Carranza, whose attitude toward the United States was not unfriendly. The dissident Mexican revolutionary Francisco Villa, often called "Pancho," became increasingly hostile toward the United States after Woodrow Wilson recognized the Carranza administration. Villa began a campaign of intimidation against the Americans, apparently hoping he could provoke United States intervention in his country and thus injure the reputation of his political opponents.[3]

In March 1916 Villa raided the town of Columbus, New Mexico. In retaliation Wilson dispatched a punitive expedition into Mexico under the command of General John J. Pershing. This military force had the halfhearted approval of the Mexican government, although Carranza had apparently envisioned a smaller detachment of troops engaged in hot pursuit of marauders across the border. Mutual misunderstandings and irritations multiplied between the two countries until they had inadvertently maneuvered themselves into a delicate and potentially dangerous situation. Wilson managed to avoid an unnecessary war, but for a time tensions remained extremely high. As a result of these emotions, "the President on June 18 called out practically the entire National Guard . . . to protect the border."[4]

The Detroit Light Guard and the rest of the Michigan National Guard units were mobilized and would soon head to Texas to patrol the boundary with Mexico. Rapid preparations for leaving were made at the Light Guard's Brush Street Armory. Recent recruits were formed into "awkward squads" for intensive training. One sometimes encountered guardsmen drilling in hurriedly assembled semblances of uniforms that included "civilian trousers with an O.D. Army shirt. . . . There were only one or two rifles for every squad of recruits." The new volunteers who flocked to fill the vacancies in the Light Guard were attracted not only by the opportunities for immediate service on the border but also by the chance to enter a unit of seasoned citizen-soldiers with a highly developed sense of patriotism.[5]

In a short time the Light Guardsmen and the other members of their National Guard regiment were prepared to leave for the Southwest. "At 9:00 P.M. the regimental band struck up with 'The Girl I Left Behind Me,' and the long column of the Thirty-first started on the first lap of the trip to the Mexican Border." The journey from the Brush Street Armory on 23 June, however, did not lead directly to Texas. The unit detoured for further training and organization at Grayling. There the newer members of the regiment would be introduced to the rigors of life in the field and the National Guardsmen would receive additional equipment. Supplies were so short that sometimes "three men shared one blanket." On 1 July the Thirty-first Michigan was officially mustered into federal service. The next day it paraded before Michigan's Governor Woodbridge N. Ferris, and on the third day the regiment left for El Paso, Texas, to begin its work.[6]

Arriving in El Paso on 7 July, the Michigan guardsmen camped on the elegant site once occupied by the city dump. To Michiganians the climate, the topography, and the flora and fauna of the Lone Star State were startlingly different from their home. The midwesterners responded to the situation by joking about their surroundings and poking fun at themselves by making up and singing ditties about service in Texas as foreign duty. Most of these troops, nevertheless, tolerated the undesirable conditions as part of their obligation to protect the southwestern borders of their country. One National Guardsman, however, so longed for the pine forests of Michigan that he apparently attempted to secure a medical discharge for having flat feet he had never noticed before he left Michigan. Unfortunately for this man, one of his officers had noted that he had won a foot race during some recent games in camp.[7]

The Wolverines, coming from a state rich with rivers and lakes, were not prepared for the aridity of the Southwest. They had to accustom themselves to receiving only one canteen of water a day. Sometimes marching and drilling could be so exhausting that in the evening "some of the gang waded in nearby irrigation ditches to rest their tired, aching feet." Since the troops often covered more than twelve miles a day, they deserved this small relief.[8]

Although high-minded motives impelled most of those serving on the Texas-Mexican frontier, some remuneration was indeed welcome to men pulled away from their civilian vocations. One veteran recalled, "'PAY DAY'—'PAY DAY' That's the Army bugle call our gang loved best of all." These citizen-soldiers were not well-paid mercenaries, for privates received only fifteen dollars a month. Indeed, it must have been difficult for the most conscientious of enlisted men to provide much support for their families.[9]

The Thirty-first Michigan assumed responsibilities for a section of frontier extending approximately ninety miles along the Rio Grande River in Texas as well as some of the boundary line between old Mexico and the state of New Mexico. The Wolverines were also charged with protecting a cement plant in El Paso regarded as an important manufacturing facility that might be endangered during any disorder. In addition to the troops in El Paso, many soldiers were stationed at Camp Cotton near the international border. The Michiganians, to be sure, constituted only a segment of the forces President Wilson had called into service in the Southwest.[10]

In late November the Light Guardsmen and their colleagues had a traditional Thanksgiving dinner Texas style. The food, "turkey . . . and all the fixin's," was supplemented by a storm of sand and dust that passed over Camp Cotton. But by late January 1917, the crisis with Mexico having subsided, the Michiganians returned home, and the Thirty-first Regiment was mustered out of the federal service.[11]

The National Guard had hardly arrived back in Detroit, however, when the deteriorating relations between the United States and Imperial Germany began to create a new challenge. Although the First World War had begun in Europe in August 1914, the United States had not entered the struggle. Now German military leaders, hoping to strike a decisive blow against England, France, and their allies, ordered the submarine fleet to sink merchant ships without warning. This procedure, morally repugnant to the American people, led Wilson to break diplomatic relations with Germany in February 1917. In early April the president successfully requested a declaration of war from Congress against Germany and the so-called Central Powers allied with it. As early as February a

Light Guardsman had recorded after an evening drill that a number of men had walked over to a nearby saloon for refreshments. It was just as well that they took their beer and sandwiches in a relaxed atmosphere of friendship and good conversation at their favorite watering place on Bates between Congress and Larned. For shortly they and the American nation would be plunged into the most frightful war the world had known up to that time. Soon many of those men would be headed to France, and some of them would never return. Those who did suffered fearful ordeals, although they also attained impressive achievements.[12]

After the declaration of war, mobilization of the country's armed might proceeded rapidly, and the federal government relied heavily on the National Guard to serve as the nucleus for new units it assembled for the expeditionary force it would send overseas to aid America's hard-pressed allies. On 18 July the War Department created the Thirty-second Division based on state troops called into service from Michigan and Wisconsin, including all of those who had seen action on the Mexican border in 1916.[13]

During the Great War the Detroit Light Guard served as the 125th Infantry Regiment in the crack Thirty-second, which became one of the most notable units in the American Expeditionary Force. The division became known by its insignia, which contained a red arrow. So remarkable were the achievements of this group in the fighting on the western front that newspapers often observed that it cut through the German lines like a red arrow. The Thirty-second's prowess on the battlefield so impressed the French that one of their generals eventually christened its soldiers "Les Terribles."[14]

As the Light Guardsmen and other National Guard units prepared to enter the United States Army, every effort was expended to secure additional recruits. Local leaders energetically urged Detroiters to volunteer for military service. Special "Four-Minute Men" eloquently applied their talents to mobilize the local population's support for the war effort. Among the outstanding orators who helped arouse a patriotic fervor was Frank Murphy, who in future years would occupy a number of key public offices including mayor of Detroit, governor of Michigan, and justice of the United States Supreme Court. In Detroit, in Michigan, and throughout the United States, citizens rallied behind President Wilson in the country's campaign not only to defeat Imperial Germany but also to "make the world safe for democracy." The Wolverine troops who traveled to Camp MacArthur at Waco, Texas, to join the Thirty-second Division left Detroit in an atmosphere of fervent support and encouragement.[15]

At Camp MacArthur the National Guardsmen from Michigan were organized into the Sixty-third Brigade, including the 125th, the Detroit Light Guard, and the 126th Regiments; those from Wisconsin were organized into the Sixty-fourth Brigade. Although the troops arriving in Waco were experienced militiamen representing the best of the citizen-soldiers from their respective states, they still required a thorough training program. The men of the Thirty-second had to prepare to face some of the finest battle-hardened armies in the world. The United States military was aided in these efforts by veteran French and British liaison officers familiar with conditions on the western front. In the arid fields of Texas the American troops even dug trenches to simulate the type of warfare conducted in Europe.[16]

To be effective a fighting unit has to have a special sense of coherence and élan. Aiming to create such an esprit de corps, the Thirty-second formed a football team during training. The Red Arrow's eleven played a challenging schedule, and its success foreshadowed the division's special achievements on the battlefield. The football team went through its regular season of vying with other service teams undefeated and then crushed the Oklahoma A & M Varsity 39 to 0. Following this victory the players received an invitation to travel to Detroit to meet the University of Detroit's football powerhouse at Navin Field, predecessor to Tiger Stadium. In this game on 1 December, the division team, tired by the long train ride and contending with an outstanding foe, lost 27 to 7. There was solace, however, for the losers, for both groups of players were afterwards entertained by members of the Detroit Athletic Club. Four days later the Thirty-second's athletes defeated by a score of 20 to 0 the strong team of the Michigan Agricultural College, the precursor of Michigan State University.[17]

By late 1917 inspectors from the War Department had judged that the group had achieved an advanced stage of preparation that enabled it to be sent to Europe. Major General James Parker had been in charge of the division during its initial training, but he received a transfer in December 1917. Brigadier General William G. Haan took his place and guided the unit through its wartime service in France. By January 1918 members of the Thirty-second had begun their move to Camp Merritt in New Jersey in preparation for their transit overseas. As they left Texas the local newspapers affectionately referred to the midwesterners as "Waco's Own" and closely and sympathetically followed their campaigns in Europe. During its voyage to France the division suffered its first casualties of the war. A German submarine torpedoed the troopship *Tuscania* early in February, and thirteen of the soldiers lost their lives.[18]

As the men of the Thirty-second landed in France they were surprised and dejected to learn that their unit had been "designated as a replacement organization for the First Army Corps." Such a plan meant that instead of going into battle as a cohesive group, the members of the division would simply be utilized as substitutes for battlefield casualties in other units. Nothing could have been more damaging to the pride of a well-trained outfit with a zest for its mission. In the judgment of its commander, the Thirty-second had already achieved a "fighting spirit" prior to its arrival but "the heart was taken out of the men" when they learned they could not go into combat together. General Haan successfully exerted every effort to have his command's status as a replacement unit reversed. Of particular importance to the Detroit Light Guard, the general was also able to have the 125th Infantry Regiment returned to the Red Arrow Division from special service as "labor troops."[19]

The Thirty-second rapidly restored its fighting edge and prepared to go into battle. The troops undertook more intensive training to ready themselves for the harsh and special conditions of warfare on the western front. In the spring of 1918 General Ludendorff, the German commander, was able to transfer numerous divisions from the eastern front because Russia had been knocked out of the war. The Germans, consequently, had the manpower to begin an offensive at a time when the British and French were starting to feel the cumulative effects of three years of savage bloodletting. The Allies desperately needed the soldiers the United States could supply. The able commander of the American Expeditionary Force, General John J. Pershing, insisted that his troops be used not just as a pool of replacements for Anglo-French armies but that American units of significant size fight on the battlefield together. Thus, in April 1918 the authorities rushed to give the Thirty-second Division its final polishing and preparation for combat duty so that the midwesterners could join the fray to block the enemy attempt to knock England and France out of the war. Indeed, so pressing was the need for fresh soldiers for the Allies that Pershing and his advisers decided that the Thirty-second was ready for battle, even though it had not completed as much training as they had hoped for.[20]

As the unit moved to the front, it received mobile food equipment called "rolling kitchens" so that troops could be fed under combat conditions. In transit, for security reasons, various battalions entrained at different points, and only a few key officers knew the Thirty-second's ultimate destination. But to the doughboys, as the American soldiers were popularly called, the important issue was less their specific geographical goal than the fact that they were finally going to fight the enemy.

The first engagement of the unit was in Alsace, a province which Germany had seized at the end of the Franco-Prussian War in 1871. Hence, the Red Arrow Division became the first group of Americans to penetrate Imperial German territory during the Great War, only one of the many distinctions the midwesterners would achieve before the Armistice in 1918.[21]

The first troops of the Thirty-second began to arrive in the Alsatian sector on 18 May, relieving some weary French veterans. By the middle of June the remainder of the unit had moved into position on that front. The division obtained its first combat experience, although it did not take part in widespread operations. The men did adapt to the conditions of the battlefield, where every moment could involve a situation in which judgment and skill determined the difference between life and death. During this period the midwesterners engaged largely in the fighting between patrols clashing in no-man's-land, the area which lay between the trenches of the two armies and which was controlled by neither side. By the middle of July the Thirty-second had suffered 368 casualties but had acquired invaluable, albeit costly, experience in the deadly thrust and counter-thrust in which it had been engaged. The United States forces had transformed the fighting in Alsace. When the Americans arrived in the sector both the German and the French troops had become so exhausted that they were reluctant to join in battle. The doughboys, however, threw themselves into the struggle with such vigor that their area of the front soon became one of the most hotly contested ones. Indeed, as early as late May a member of the unit recorded, "The first German raiding party to inflict casualty in hand-to-hand combat . . . came across No Man's Land during the night." As the fighting continued, "observation balloon[s] were used by both sides during the day. During the night both sides used patrols and kept No Man's Land brilliantly lighted with flares."[22]

Given the inconclusive nature of the struggle in the Alsatian sector, the now-experienced men of the Thirty-second felt that they ought to be used for more challenging assignment. When General Pershing inspected them in July, General Haan expressed the unit's desire for greater responsibilities. The A.E.F. commander replied, "I like the snap in your Division, and unless I am mistaken you will be on your way to a more active front in the very near future. Tell your men I like their spirit." Pershing's visit and compliments created an almost electric atmosphere of eagerness in the division. Thoughtful members of the Thirty-second sensed that they were moving on to another stage in their assignment, even though they realized the many theories circulating about their next destination simply involved the fanciful speculations of the rumor mill. Where they might end up on the "big front," as the men called the crucial area of fighting, was not clear, but the Red Arrow troops were prepared to do their part.[23]

At the end of July, without knowing their journey's end, the men of the Thirty-second entrained in the beautiful midsummer sunshine and headed toward Paris. Some of the troops passed through the city in the daytime, and one of the soldiers observed, "As the toy French engines jerked the toy French box-cars through the outskirts of the French capital the people in the street stopped and waved at us. They crowded the windows of the buildings and shouted 'Vive L'Americain!' and the doughboys yelled back in good American fashion."[24]

The railroad journey for the Thirty-second ended on 24 July, a symbolic date for the Detroiters in the unit because it was the day on which the French had founded their city in 1701. Almost immediately the division proceeded by truck into the area of Château-Thierry. Here the Red Arrow troops became attached to the Thirty-eighth Corps of the French Sixth Army. The doughboys took up billets in tiny towns and villages scattered throughout the vicinity. The region exhibited numerous signs of the destruction caused by the recent, savage fighting that had forced a German retreat. Helmets and other, more grisly, souvenirs of battle lay scattered all over the area. The men of the Thirty-second had finally reached their ultimate goal, the "big front." Those of the midwesterners who could not find a billet with the local population had to make do with pup tents or else took shelter in "wrecked buildings and hoped it wouldn't rain." In the distant sky, the soldiers could see the ominous lightning of the "red flashes" produced by thundering artillery.[25]

As they munched on cold rations, the rolling kitchens having not yet arrived, the men must have been sobered by the realization of how close they were to the western front's version of Armageddon. The midwesterners in their olive drab uniforms took over the sector of "the Foret de Fere, near le Charmel" at 11:00 A.M., 30 July 1918. The doughboys from Michigan and Wisconsin soon found themselves involved in the most difficult fighting they had ever encountered. The Imperial German Army once again attempted a knockout blow against the Allies. For eight days the soldiers of the Thirty-second fought like battle-hardened veterans in the Aisne-Marne offensive. They played a vital role by providing crucial aid in driving "the German line . . . steadily back, over difficult ground, . . . for a distance of 19 kilometers." This represented a tremendous accomplishment for the American newcomers who had replaced the experienced but exhausted troops of the French Third Division.[26]

In particular, the Michigan contingent went into action the night of 30 July and the early hours of the next day. Like their comrades of the Wisconsin Sixty-fourth Brigade, the Wolverines of the Sixty-third achieved notable success in the battle. Detroit's Light Guardsmen and their colleagues showed themselves to be among the best of the American Expeditionary Force in that offensive at the end of July and the beginning of August. They were able to overcome strong enemy resistance at such heavily fortified places as Hill 212, "a hornet's nest of German machine guns." In the "hot work and . . . wicked fighting" in moving against a well-entrenched, skillful, and tenacious foe, the Light Guardsmen and their comrades of the Thirty-second Division performed effectively as well as courageously in the face of horrendous opposition. Although it was a bloody war in which men were killing each other using the latest technology, "'runners,' . . . courageous and active little" doughboys, still carried information to and from the front lines when other, more formal, means of communication failed. These intrepid soldiers had to pass through "the hidden mesh of barbed wire" time and time again on their missions.[27]

On 3 August, despite heavy enemy shelling, the men of the Thirty-second had regrouped behind the cover of a conveniently located shelter about daybreak. "All units were deployed by 9:00 A.M. and a general advance got underway with the 125th Infantry as Brigade advance guard." This group of Light Guardsmen drove on to a point near the Vesle River. As they moved up they had an almost panoramic view of the battlefield. The retreating Germans destroyed "bridges and vast stores of their war material." About two kilometers south of the river at a point where the terrain, including a ravine and some accompanying heights, formed a particularly defensible bastion for the enemy, a ferocious barrage of machine gun and artillery fire temporarily forced the doughboys "to halt and dig in." The pause was a brief one, however. The men of the Thirty-second again struggled forward, overcoming fierce German resistance. At great cost the midwesterners relentlessly drove the foe back to the Vesle River.[28]

On the night of 6 August and on the morning of the next day, the exhausted men of the Red Arrow Division were relieved by troops from other units. As they caught up on their sleep and recovered from the battle, the members of the Thirty-second for the first time began to realize the magnitude of their achievement. In their initial large-scale action on the western front, they had contended with and defeated some of the elite of the German forces, including the crack Fourth Prussian Guards. Not surprisingly, General Haan exhibited ebullient spirits as he visited the division. Said one doughboy of the commander, "The Old Boy was all smiles. I guess he's satisfied."[29]

The general had reason to be so satisfied. The Light Guardsmen and their Red Arrow comrades had been relatively inexperienced when they had gone into battle against the German veterans, who represented one of the world's finest military traditions. The Americans had conducted themselves with distinction. Their success, however, had been at a fearful cost; they had suffered four thousand casualties in the Aisne-Marne campaign. The brutal results had affected both sides: the unit's "burial squads interred more German dead than the 32nd Division's total of killed and missing."[30]

This campaign earned the unit its French sobriquet. When the commander of the Thirty-eighth French Corps viewed the manner in which the Red Arrows had advanced against some of the finest units of the Imperial German Army, he exclaimed, "Oui, Oui, *Les soldats terrible*, tres bien, tres bien!" From this admiring characterization came "Les Terribles," the affectionate name by which the French continued to refer to the Thirty-second.[31]

After a short period of rest and after receiving some replacement troops who readily absorbed the spirit of the unit, the Thirty-second joined the French Tenth Army headed by General Charles Mangin. This leader, one of the most distinguished of the Gallic officers, enthusiastically welcomed "Les Terribles" to his command. Soon the midwesterners again moved toward the front, with the greater assurance of veterans who had been tested in a ferocious battle. This time, however, they would be engaged in a more relentless kind of struggle, the Oise-Aisne campaign.[32]

On 27 August, the Thirty-second Division took over a section of the front. At 2:00 A.M. the Sixty-third Brigade relieved the exhausted 127th French Division. The Gallic army had planned an attack for 7:00 that morning, the exact time that General Haan would take command of the sector. Despite the fact that the offensive was to take place at an awkward moment of transition, Haan insisted that the Red Arrow Division was fully prepared for the engagement. Thus, the Michiganians went into action with the first wave of attacking troops. Although the Wolverines had only five hours of rest before they "went over the top for the first clash of what was to be a continuous struggle for five bloody days," their fatigue did not impair their effectiveness. This first stage of the Oise-Aisne drive took place at a village near Soissons called Juvigny.[33]

The second day of the campaign began after an all-night downpour of rain and German shells. The "shellholes were soon mudholes." In general, the terrain around Juvigny gave the enemy a large number of naturally strong defensive positions. The men of the Red Arrow Division were to serve "as a shock unit." The division's "mission was to smash the strong German resistance which was holding up the French advance." The attack of the American troops in this battle involved overcoming capable opposition under difficult conditions. One officer wrote that "the French tanks were constantly stalling and drew artillery fire. . . . The 125th Headquarters sent Captain Lamb over to our position to locate the machine gun nests and clean them out with one pounders." This soldier moments later was killed in the action. In the captured the awesome enemy citadel of the Kriemhilde Stellung. These achievements cost the division, however, the brutal price of more than six thousand casualties.[40]

Such, then, were the accomplishments and sacrifices of the Red Arrows as they left the battlefield on 20 October for a respite from their grim and savage labors. Their place of rest hardly constituted elegant facilities. The division had to stay in crude shelters, dug-outs in the ground, that had been designed for twenty-four hundred troops but which had to accommodate the eighteen thousand exhausted veterans of the Thirty-second. Many of the dug-outs contained considerable amounts of water, and each of them was heavily infested with the distressing body lice the doughboys called "cooties."[41]

Still, after the many weary days of battle, the shelters, with their attendant cooties, water, and lack of space, did constitute some relief. General Haan visited the various units of the division in their rude retreats, showing his concern and good humor. The fatherly commander assured his men that with their help the Allies "had the Germans 'on-the-run'" and that soon the conflict would result in victory. Then the general vowed, recalls one doughboy, "to take us back to an excellent REST CAMP just as soon as the war was over. But . . . there would be absolutely NO REST FOR ANYONE until the Germans were willing to admit the defeat which was already upon them." In a few days, therefore, "Les Terribles," refreshed by their brief leave from the front and refitted with new uniforms and equipment, readied themselves to return to battle.[42]

On 1 November the Thirty-second Division was transferred from the Fifth to the Third United States Army Corps as part of the preparations to move once again against the Germans. The enemy still remained ensconced in strong positions east of the Meuse River. On 5 November "Les Terribles" crossed the river on a pontoon bridge under the cover of darkness. The men of the Red Arrow Division had anticipated that they would enter a sector of retreating Germans. At the end of October the enemy had begun to collapse, plagued in some areas by desertions from their hitherto well-disciplined army. When the troops of the Thirty-second, however, reached the foggy east side of the Meuse, they found themselves in the midst not of a crumbling Teutonic army but of a well-organized German force determined to fight fiercely to hold onto its carefully prepared positions. A tremendously bitter struggle followed. The midwesterners, though badly exposed, conducted themselves with the bravery and skill for which they had become renowned. Regrouping in spite of a savage raking from enemy guns, the Thirty-second continued to press its charge against the last-ditch defense of the Imperial German Army. The division's officers had planned an attack for 7:00 on the morning of 11 November.[43]

Meanwhile, even the leaders of the once seemingly invincible German war machine realized the grim game in which they were engaged was lost. Order at home in Germany began to dissolve into chaos as discipline disintegrated in the country's military forces. His own generals reluctantly convinced Kaiser Wilhelm II that he would have to abdicate. These leaders sued for an armistice and, although shocked at the harsh terms upon which the Allied commander Marshall Foch insisted, they had no choice. "Very early on the morning of the 11th the Germans filed into Foch's railway command car, sat down quietly, and signed the papers. The ceasefire came into effect at eleven o'clock that morning."[44]

As the events occurred, it was not at all clear to the men in the lines, such as the members of the Thirty-second, how close they were to peace and the end of the savage carnage. On their section of the front the resistance of the enemy continued to the very end. One soldier of the unit recorded on the eve of the Armistice that reports of the Germans retreating were "erroneous. . . . A heavy artillery fire was kept up during the night of November 10–11 and this increased in volume during the early morning hours of November 11th." Just before the division was supposed to launch its attack at 7:00 A.M., the unit's headquarters cancelled it. The German barrage, however, continued until the moment the Armistice became effective. The chaplain of the 125th Infantry was fatally wounded shortly before the cease-fire. When the guns stopped there was for a time simply "stunned silence." Soon, as the soldiers realized the threat of imminent death had been lifted and victory achieved, an exuberant mood overtook them. They built huge bonfires and celebrated as word spread, "FINIS LA GUERRE!"[45]

The Armistice was an agreement to stop fighting, but it did not create the final peace. Indeed, negotiations to formally end the war did not begin until the following year. The resulting settlement, the Treaty of Versailles, although heavily influenced by President Wilson, was rejected by the United States Senate. Consequently, the United States had to arrange separate pacts with Germany and her allies. In November 1918 it would be a long time before the war would end in a de jure as well as a de facto sense.[46]

In the meantime, the Allied leaders felt they had to provide an army of occupation for some areas of Germany to ensure that there would be no renewal of fighting. The Thirty-second Division, as part of the United States Third Army, served in this capacity. During the movement into the former enemy's territory, General Haan was assigned to the command of the Seventh Army Corps and General William Lassiter assumed direction of the Red Arrow Division. Haan's devotion to "Les Terribles" continued after he left them. He retained a keen interest in their welfare, often corresponding with the parents of deceased or missing soldiers of the unit.[47]

After a long and rigorous march, the Thirty-second reached the Rhine just one month after the signing of the Armistice. Although some of the troops arrived with blistered, even bleeding, feet, on the whole their health and their spirits were excellent. At Koblenz the Red Arrow unit occupied the front line in the German territory controlled by the United States Third Army. In the course of their garrison duties, the bitter emotions of war rapidly subsided and an amiable relationship developed between the members of the Thirty-second and the local population within the limits of and sometimes in spite of the no-fraternization orders of the American military. Nevertheless, restlessness increased among "Les Terribles," and most of the men longed for civilian life. In mid-February 1919 they learned that they would be shipped home by the end of May. Actually, most of them were able to return to the United States between 1 and 15 May. Although many of the units of the division disembarked at New York, some landed at Boston, and all received an enthusiastic welcome. Although the division was dissolved after the war, such an esprit de corps had developed among its members that they formed a special Thirty-second Division Veteran Association. This organization would perpetuate the Thirty-second's memory and its sense of tradition in "the years to come," with particular stress on "the spirit which led Les Terribles to success on the battlefields of France in the great year of 1918."[48]

Notes

1. Doris B. McLaughlin, *Michigan Labor: A Brief History from 1818 to the Present* (Ann Arbor, Mich., 1970), 83–85.
2. Corporal Tanglefoot [pseud.], "Our Military Ancestry," diary, DAC, typescript.
3. Arthur S. Link, *Woodrow Wilson and the Progressive Era, 1910–1917* (New York, 1954), 136.
4. Ibid., 136–40.
5. Tanglefoot, 19, 21 June 1916, DAC.
6. Ibid., 23, 24, 26 June and 1, 2, 3, 7 July 1916.
7. Ibid., 7, 8, 10, 14 July and 4, 16 August 1916.
8. Ibid., 2, 3 Oct. 1916.
9. Ibid., 12 Sept. 1916.
10. Ibid., 13, 14, 28, 29 Sept. 1916.
11. Ibid., 30 Nov. 1916, and 18, 20 Jan. 1917.
12. Ibid., 6 Feb. 1917.
13. Joint War History Commissions of Michigan and Wisconsin, *The 32nd Division in the World War, 1917–1919* (Madison, Wis., 1920), 27.
14. *Detroit Journal*, 27 Aug. 1921; Joint War History Commissions, 12–13, 70–71.
15. Tanglefoot, 27 May (quoting *Detroit News*), 30 July, 12 Aug., 29 Sept. 1917, DAC.
16. Joint War History Commissions, 27–31; Tanglefoot, 5, 21, 26 Nov. 1916, DAC.
17. Tanglefoot, 6 Oct., 24 Nov., and 1, 5 Dec. 1917, DAC.
18. Joint War History Commissions, 28, 32–33; Tanglefoot, 16, 19, 25 Jan., 5 Feb. 1918, DAC; *Detroit Journal*, 27 Aug. 1921.
19. Joint War History Commissions, 34–36, 196; *Detroit Journal*, 27 Aug. 1921.
20. Joint War History Commissions, 35–41; James L. Stokesbury, *A Short History of World War I* (New York, 1981), 261–63.
21. Joint War History Commissions, 41.
22. Ibid., 43–44; Tanglefoot, 27 May, 16 June 1918, DAC.
23. Joint War History Commissions, 49–50.
24. Ibid., 51–52.
25. Ibid., 53.
26. Ibid., 54–55.
27. Ibid., 58–59; Tanglefoot, 30, 31 July, and 1 Aug. 1918, DAC.
28. Tanglefoot, 3, 4 Aug. 1918, DAC; Joint War History Commissions, 63–67.

29. Joint War History Commissions, 67–70.

30. Ibid., 71.

31. Ibid., 70.

32. Ibid., 72–74; Tanglefoot, 23, 24 Aug. 1918, DAC.

33. Joint War History Commissions, 74–77.

34. Tanglefoot, 28, 29 Aug. 1918, DAC; Joint War History Commissions, 79–83.

35. Joint War History Commissions, 83–85.

36. Ibid., 88.

37. Ibid., 88–93; Tanglefoot, 30 Sept. 1918, DAC.

38. Joint War History Commissions, 97; Tanglefoot, 30 Sept., and 1 Oct. 1918, DAC; Stokesbury, 289.

39. Stokesbury, 282–83, 290–91; Joint War History Commissions, 98–102.

40. Joint War History Commissions, 102–15.

41. Ibid., 113–18.

42. Ibid., 118–20; Tanglefoot, 26 Oct. 1918, DAC.

43. Joint War History Commissions, 120–24; Stokesbury, 291–92.

44. Stokesbury, 305–7.

45. Tanglefoot, 10, 11 Nov. 1918, DAC; Joint War History Commissions, 124.

46. Stokesbury, 309–16.

47. Joint War History Commissions, 127–29.

48. Ibid., 130–45.

View in 1915 of the Larned and Brush Armory, which had been completed in 1898. Photographer: Charles Brewer. (Courtesy of the Burton Historical Collection, Detroit Public Library.)

Colonel Cornelius Gardener, commander of the
Thirty-first Michigan, circa 1898. (Courtesy of the
Detroit Historical Museum.)

Major Charles W. Harrah, who assumed command of the Second
Battalion, Thirty-first Michigan, in May 1898. (Courtesy of the
Detroit Historical Museum.)

Officers of the Thirty-first Michigan at Savannah, Georgia, May 1899. Photographer: Wilson. (Courtesy of the
Detroit Historical Museum.)

Company K, Thirty-first Michigan Infantry, at Tampa, Florida, circa 1898. (Courtesy of the Frank E. Storer Collection.)

Private Isaac Van Sycle, Company K, Thirty-first Michigan, at Camp Thomas, Chickamauga, Georgia, in 1898. Photographer: W. T. Barnum. (Courtesy of the Frank E. Storer Collection.)

Company M, Thirty-third Michigan, at Island Lake in 1898. (Courtesy of the Detroit Historical Museum.)

Thirty-first Michigan encampment at Camp Poland, near Knoxville, Tennessee, on New Year's Day, 1899. (Courtesy of the Detroit Historical Museum.)

Detroit Light Infantry on Woodward Avenue, circa 1900. (Courtesy of the Detroit Historical Museum.)

Band of the First Infantry, Michigan National Guard, circa 1900. (Courtesy of the Detroit Historical Museum.)

Company A of the Detroit Light Guard as Company A of the First Infantry, Michigan National Guard, circa 1903. Photographer: Shemild. (Courtesy of the Frank E. Storer Collection.)

Brigadier General Henry M. Duffield, circa 1900.
Photographic restoration by Frank E. Storer. (Courtesy of the Detroit Historical Museum.)

Ribbon and cover of the program for the celebration of the fiftieth year of the reorganization of the Detroit Light Guard, Detroit's oldest militia unit. Photographer: Frank E. Storer. (Courtesy of the Detroit Historical Museum.)

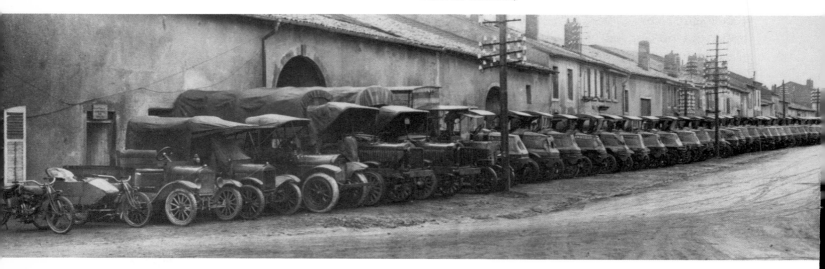

Military vehicles in a motor park, location unknown, circa 1917. (Courtesy of the 225th Infantry Archives.)

Light Guardsmen of the 125th Infantry at Sentheim, Alsace, 29 May 1918. Photographer: United States Army Signal Corps. (Courtesy of the 225th Infantry Archives.)

Detroit Light Guard as part of the First Infantry, Michigan National Guard, during the Upper Peninsula copper strike of 1913. The officer in the center of the front seat is Captain George C. Waldo. Photographer: Steckbauer. (Courtesy of the Detroit Historical Museum, George Waldo Collection.)

Advanced observation post of the 125th Infantry within grenade-throwing distance of German lines near Gildwilder, Alsace, 27 June 1918. Photographer: United States Army Signal Corps. (Courtesy of the Frank E. Storer Collection.)

French tanks supporting the 125th Infantry near Juvigny, France, 29 August 1918. Photographer: United States Army Signal Corps. (Courtesy of the Frank E. Storer Collection.)

General William G. Haan and an aide study maps in a reinforced concrete dugout captured from the Germans in the Argonne Woods and used as Thirty-second Division headquarters. Photographer: United States Army Signal Corps. (Courtesy of the Frank E. Storer Collection.)

Stretcher bearers of the 125th Infantry bringing the wounded into the medical station at Courmont, France, 1 August 1918. Photographer: United States Army Signal Corps. (Courtesy of the Frank E. Storer Collection.)

Colonel Matthias A. Wiesenhoefer serves birthday cake to officers of the 125th Infantry at Camp Livingston, Louisiana, in 1941 to mark the 111th anniversary of the founding of the Detroit City Guard. The officer in the light shirt is Brigadier General Thomas Colladay, a former commander of the Light Guard. (Courtesy of the 225th Infantry Archives.)

Vehicles of the 125th Infantry refueling on the trip to Camp Beauregard, Louisiana, in October 1940. Photographer: Vincent V. Calamia. (Courtesy of the Calamia family and the Frank E. Storer Collection.)

"Chow line" as men of the 425th Infantry take a lunch break from practice at the firing range at Camp Grayling, August 1951. Photographer: William Seiter, Detroit News. (Courtesy of the 225th Infantry Archives.)

Camp Grayling in 1949. The light rectangular area above the lake was occupied by the 425th Infantry for many years during its annual training sessions. (Courtesy of the Frank E. Storer Collection.)

Color Guard of the 425th Infantry, circa 1955. Photographer: Daniel Firestone. (Courtesy of the Frank E. Storer Collection.)

Officers of the 425th Infantry Regiment, 1955, at Camp Grayling. Photographer: Daniel Firestone. (Courtesy of the Frank E. Storer Collection.)

Staff officers of the First Battle Group, 225th Infantry, at Camp Grayling in 1959. Photographer: Firestone. (Courtesy of the Frank E. Storer Collection.)

Michigan Governor G. Mennen Williams flanked by Major General Gordon Mac-Donald (left), Colonel Ford D. McParland (right), and the Regimental Pipe Band of the 425th Infantry in 1958. Photographer: Firestone. (Courtesy of the Frank E. Storer Collection.)

Practice in using an Anti-tank recoilless rifle in the Goodison, Michigan, Training Area, circa 1953. (Courtesy of the 225th Infantry Archives.)

Cornerstone laying for the East Eight Mile Road Light Guard Armory, 14 December 1956. Secretary of the Army Wilbur M. Brucker, holding the trowel, is assisted by Walker L. Cisler, of the Armory Citizens' Committee. Photographer: Frank E. Storer. (Courtesy of the Storer-Spellman Studio.)

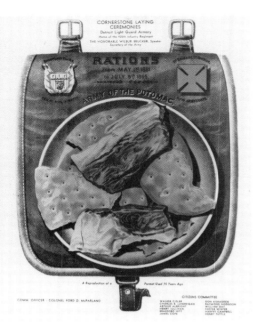

Program commemorating the laying of the cornerstone. Photographer: Frank E. Storer. (Courtesy of the Frank E. Storer Collection.)

Ford D. McParland,
Colonel, Infantry,
Commanding, 425th Infantry Regiment,
285 Piquette Avenue,
Detroit 2, Michigan.

Dear Colonel:

In regard to your call of the 28th of September and pertaining to the permission of use of the Light Guard's insignia of the Tiger head and the name "Tiger's" to the Detroit Baseball Club.-

The Detroit Baseball Club approached the Light Guard for use of it's then popular insignia and "nick name" of Tigers and the Detroit Military Unit granted this priveledge.

I, being associated with the unit at the time, know the background of the incident.

Sincerely,

JOHN S. BERSEY,
Brigadier General

Detroit Light Guard and Tiger baseball. Photographer: Frank E. Storer. (Courtesy of the 225th Infantry Archives.)

The East Eight Mile Road Light Guard Armory in 1986. Photographer: Frank E. Storer. (Courtesy of the Frank E. Storer Collection.)

Department of the Army

This is to certify that the

225TH INFANTRY

Whose special designation has become traditional through its many years of loyal, faithful, and distinguished service, is herewith recognized as having earned the honor and right to the

Traditional Designation

DETROIT LIGHT GUARD

Given Under My Hand in the City of Washington
this **3rd** day of **June 1964**

SECRETARY OF THE ARMY

Department of the Army's confirmation of the name of the Detroit Light Guard. Photographer: Frank E. Storer. (Courtesy of Headquarters, First Battalion, 225th Infantry.)

Carved stone tiger's head that had been located in the outside wall of the corner tower of the 1898 Light Guard Armory and was placed in the lobby of the 1957 armory above a plaque dedicated to the Citizens' Committee. Photographer: Frank E. Storer. (Courtesy of the Frank E. Storer Collection.)

Light Guard Distinguished Service Medal, established 1950. Lapel pin and rosettes are also shown. Photographer: Frank E. Storer. (Courtesy of the 225th Infantry Archives.)

Coat of Arms of the Detroit Light Guard. Artist: Frank E. Storer. (Courtesy of the Frank E. Storer Collection.)

Brigadier General Stanley J. Wilk, the only member of the post-World War II Michigan National Guard to rise through the ranks to become a general. On 1 September 1983 he was assigned deputy commander of the State Area Readiness Command and promoted to brigadier general of the National Guard of the United States. Photographer: Frank E. Storer. (Courtesy of the Frank E. Storer Collection.)

Ford D. McParland in a portrait made in January 1960. The original photograph showed him with a colonel's insignia, but upon his retirement he was promoted to brigadier general; consequently, the picture was altered to show the new rank. Photograph made and retouched by Frank E. Storer. (Courtesy of the Frank E. Storer Collection.)

7

From the Great War to the Space Age

The United States had entered the struggle in 1917 thinking that this was the war to end all wars. While the country demobilized, the American people, or at least a great many of them, believed that their recent crusade marked the beginning of a period of permanent international tranquility. This feeling may have added to the understandable eagerness of the veterans to return to their civilian pursuits. The Light Guardsmen exhibited the same high spirits when they left to serve in the struggle to make the world safe for democracy in 1917 as they did in May 1919 at Camp Custer, Michigan, when they were demobilized from the federal service. They, however, continued in their role as citizen-soldiers. In December 1920 they were reorganized as the First Battalion of the First Infantry of the Michigan National Guard while remaining part of the Thirty-second Division. In November of 1921 the Detroiters were then redesignated as the First Battalion of the 125th Infantry.[1]

In the decade that followed, when Americans hoped that finally swords would be beaten into plowshares, committed professionals in the regular army and navy, as well as dedicated citizen-soldiers in the National Guard, kept alive the traditions of military preparedness in case the noble dream should prove an illusion and the nation should once more require a strong right arm to defend itself. During the 1920s the Harding administration implemented a major limitation of naval armaments at the 1921–22 Washington Conference, and the United States together with France sponsored the Kellogg-Briand Pact, which renounced war as an instrument of national policy. This agreement was signed by most nations of the world. One cynical United States senator sneered at the understanding as an "international kiss," and, indeed,

American Secretary of State Frank B. Kellogg backed the treaty largely for its public relations value rather than because of a belief in its efficacy. Many of his fellow citizens also doubted the practicality of the pact, even though such a stance appealed to the country's widespread idealism at this time.[2]

It was in such an atmosphere of indifference to the necessity for military preparations to defend the country that organizations such as the Light Guard performed a very constructive role in carrying on the traditions of the voluntary militia. The followers of the Tiger's Head were training men and officers who would help the United States greatly when a largely disarmed nation would have to prepare rapidly for the whirlwind of World War II. During the 1920s the members of the Light Guard demonstrated a strong sense of their history. As the group's records reveal, "In the fall of 1922 at the suggestion of Major Alma Lake a meeting was called to consider a getting together of some of the Light Guard Boys for the 16th of Nov. the 67th Anniversary of the Guard. Enthusiasm was shown from the start and when the Dinner was held at the Army-Navy Club 154 members were present." The congenial gathering of the veterans that day was used to form a "permanent organization" to be called the Old Detroit Light Guard. Officers selected included General Charles W. Harrah as president and Robert E. Mason as secretary.[3]

Later, in 1929, a leading Detroit journalist, Ken Laub, devoted his column "Listening in on Detroit" to an appreciation of a gathering of the Old Detroit Light Guard that had been held at the Book Cadillac Hotel. Generations of Detroit history seemed to have paraded in front of the writer's eyes as he observed the meeting. In speaking of a resolution determining who could join the Old Detroit Light Guard, Laub wrote, "Though ineligible to membership, . . . I speak with enthusiasm of this resolution (truly epoch-marking in the social and civic life of Detroit and in the lives of all who cherish Detroit's fine old traditions), because to any sympathetic outside observer who has had the peculiar privilege of attending . . . a reunion of the Old Detroit Light Guard, it would seem a pity—almost a public catastrophe—that these annual reunions should come to an end." Detroit's senior organization of citizen-soldiers, then, more than ever had become a distinctive, even unique, institution in the life of the city in the twentieth century.[4]

"Gen. Charles W. Harrah presided," Laub's account continues. "Col. John S. Bersey was the principal speaker. Secretary Robert E. Mason did all the work. Private Henry H. James, 84 years old, oldest living member of the organization . . . sat beside General Harrah and lent an attentive ear to the stories told by his fellow-guardsmen." From a private who had enlisted in 1861 to a general who had provided leadership for Detroit's militia over the years to a colonel who one day would be a general and who already had begun a generation's service as adjutant general of Michigan, all of those at the head table as well as the entire two hundred present at that meeting seemed to the reporter to blend together the military past and future of Detroit.[5]

In the 1920s with its heightened pride in its long and honorable past and a continuing sense of community responsibility, the organization under the leadership of General Harrah turned over the bulk of the records of the Brady Guards, Light Guard, and Light Infantry to the Burton Historical Collection of the Detroit Public Library. The guards felt that both their successors in the militia and the other people of the area would benefit from the preservation and availability of the records.[6]

At the beginning of the next decade, half-way between its participation in two world wars, the militia marked the diamond anniversary of its use of the name Light Guard. The celebrations and reminiscences on this occasion were marked by articles in Detroit's two leading newspapers.[7] As the organization and the community observed the senior militia unit's jubilee, however, the world suffered a depression, the most severe in the history of civilization. In the United States this economic crisis emphasized the tendency of Americans to become preoccupied with matters within their own borders and to sometimes turn away from concern about international affairs and national defense. Events, nevertheless, forced the American people and their leaders to address the growing challenge abroad of a rearmed Germany. Controlled by the totalitarian Nazis who wished to use armed might to dominate the world with a thousand-year *reich*, Germany and her allies, Fascist Italy and the expanding and militaristic Imperial Japan, threatened the stability of a democratic world order and ultimately the security of the United States itself.[8]

In 1931 Japan seized the Chinese province of Manchuria and within a few years began the attempt to subdue the rest of that country. In 1936 Italy conquered the African nation of Ethiopia, whose armed forces lacked the equipment to fight a modern war. In 1938 Germany compelled Austria to unite with it and in the same year began the process of brutally devouring the hapless republic of Czechoslovakia. Then in 1939 the Nazi troops invaded Poland. England and France, fulfilling their treaty obligations, declared war against the Teutonic aggressor, and World War II began. Germany not only crushed Poland, geographically far removed from its allies, but also occupied Denmark and Norway in 1940 and then used superiority in tanks and airplanes to overwhelm the Netherlands and Belgium. Next the Nazis swept around the end of the famed French defenses of the Maginot Line, crushing the resistance of the Gallic nation whose once proud six-million-man army had been regarded as the finest in the world at the beginning of the war.[9]

As France crumbled, a British expeditionary force barely escaped from that country, assisted by weather that hindered the Luftwaffe, the German air corps. The soldiers, trapped on the beaches of Dunkirk, were saved by a fleet of English boats that ferried the men back to the beleaguered island, which braced itself for a possible invasion by the troops of Germany's dictator, Adolf Hitler. United States President Franklin D. Roosevelt rallied the support of an increasingly alarmed American public and its representatives in Congress behind a dual policy of augmenting national defense as well as providing aid for the gallant British. The latter carried on the struggle alone for a time, led by the great wartime leader Winston Churchill, who had become prime minister in one of the darkest moments in his country's history.[10]

In September 1940, in the wake of the fall of France, President Roosevelt began to federalize the National Guard, and the process was completed by the following June. This aided the rapid buildup of the United States Army in perhaps the most perilous time in the nation's history since the secession crisis of 1860–61. Of course, Roosevelt's action affected the Light Guard.[11] Citizen-soldiers in units such as the 125th Infantry comprised one of the few organizations in the country continually engaged in the task of maintaining military preparedness for any struggle for national safety and world peace. As international events gradually had their impact on the consciousness of Americans, however, the country's thinking began to shift from the crisis at home to the perils abroad.[12]

In 1937 the Light Guard applied its professional skills and reputation for integrity in a tense situation in Michigan. The depression decade was a period of growing unionization in the United States, and the reluctance of management to grant workers their legal right of collective bargaining through representatives of their own choosing exacerbated industrial strife. At the end of December 1936 General Motors employees in Flint, Michigan, began a sit-down strike at the Fisher Body No. 1 and No. 2 plants. The strike, in which the protesting workers refused to leave their employer's premises, led to an especially complex legal and emotional tangle. Court orders were not obeyed by workers who felt that management ignored the rights of union members. Many individuals of good will became more interested in seeing a peaceful resolution of the situation than in applying the technicalities of the law. Indeed, members of the Fisher family begged Michigan's chief executive to do everything in his power to avoid bloodshed so that their name would not be sullied by such a tragedy.[13]

Governor Frank Murphy, also anxious to avoid violence, called out units of the Michigan National Guard, including the 125th, in January 1937, and they began to arrive "in force in Flint on January 13. 'Equipped with all the panoply of war,' the Flint *Journal* reported on that date, 'armed forces of the state of Michigan took command of the tense situation . . . today.' The strikers . . . were delighted [with the arrival of the Guard] because they saw the troops as 'the arm of the governor,' whom they trusted."[14]

Colonel Joseph H. Lewis led these military forces. He was "commander of the 119th Field Artillery, a seasoned, unaggressive soldier who had once been a tool maker in an automobile plant" and had among other experiences seen duty with the militia in its 1916 stint on the Mexican border. "In Flint, Lewis benefited from the advice of Samuel D. Pepper, a calm, deliberate man who had been judge advocate general of the state since 1908 and who was an authority on military law and the use of the Guard on riot duty." The adjutant general of Michigan at that time, who was able to supply Governor Murphy with advice about the use of the militia, was that veteran and astute Light Guard officer General John S. Bersey.[15]

The National Guardsmen conducted themselves in the best tradition of the citizen-soldier in the tense and emotional situation in Flint, observing an attitude of strict neutrality and avoiding involvement in the difficult dispute. Although the guardsmen were prepared to act in case of disorder, their presence may have facilitated Murphy's aim of "peaceful negotiation." When the troops left Flint at the conclusion of the 1937 strike, their actions "elicited a great deal of praise from responsible officials."[16]

World events in 1940 produced a perilous situation for the United States, but if the country's armed forces were in an unprepared state, the men of the Light Guard were in good condition and ready to rally to whatever tasks should be required of them. The role of the unit was to be "largely a training and cadre regiment during World War II. However, many of its officers and men saw combat in other regiments of the division."[17]

Detroit's senior militia company played a significant and constructive part in the United States struggle against the Axis powers by becoming a source of personnel for many other units. When the 125th Infantry entered the service of the United States on 15 October 1940 on the orders of the nation's commander in chief, the regiment was still part of the Thirty-second Division. As the country moved toward war, the veteran militiamen were to quickly receive additional and intensive training to prepare them for the complex and sophisticated process that modern warfare had become. The War Department at first sent the Detroiters south to Camp Beauregard, Louisiana. Ironically, the heirs of the Michigan company that had rallied to the colors so quickly when Lincoln asked for ninety-day volunteers to suppress the rebellion began their special training for World War II in a post named for a Confederate commander. The atmosphere of urgency created confusion, and the conditions for the Michiganians at their destination were less than elegant. Reported one Wolverine, "we were quartered in one of the finest mud holes to be found in Louisiana."[18]

The lack of time to prepare adequate quarters for the National Guardsmen, the swampy terrain, and the "inclement weather" produced deplorable living conditions. The facility, located a few miles from the town of Alexandria, had actually been "an old National Guard Camp which [had] been in use since before World War I." Although some parts of the area had been improved, many troops were quartered in the former rifle range, which was situated on low grounds that soon became a damp morass. The climate, to which the Michiganians were not accustomed, and the inadequate physical setting created "a great deal of illness during the fall period of 1940." Conditions were difficult not just for the 125th Infantry but for the entire Thirty-second Division, for Camp Beauregard simply was not prepared properly to house and care for so many men.[19]

The strength of the 125th soon increased from approximately fourteen hundred officers and men to almost twenty-eight hundred. Consequently, "it was during this period that many sergeants were made lieutenants bringing up the officer strength of the regiment." War or the possibility of it always provides an opportunity for individuals with leadership potential to rise to positions allowing them to make use of their abilities. Company records reveal that "most of the officers were credited with 15 years service. Few had less than ten years. Many had worked their way up from the ranks." Training continued at Camp Beauregard until February 1941, when the 125th Infantry along with the rest of the Thirty-second Division moved to nearby Camp Livingston. In the next two months, as the recently passed United States Selective Service Act went into effect, the regiment's strength was augmented, and its leadership had to devote itself to teaching the green draftees the numerous skills and procedures of military life that the more experienced National Guardsmen had acquired over the years.[20]

The men of the 125th and their comrades applied themselves to learning the martial arts as well as to making their living quarters more bearable. They prepared themselves for their duties so well that they were chosen in the summer of 1941 to participate in maneuvers the United States War Department had decided to conduct in Louisiana as part of its effort to prepare the armed forces rapidly for possible conflict. The division in these exercises served in the Third Army commanded by General Walter Krueger, whose staff included Dwight D. Eisenhower, then a lieutenant colonel. In these war games the Michiganians and their colleagues underwent hardships similar to actual battle conditions. Long afterwards the participants remembered the "many long miles which had to be marched in the heat, the chiggers, and insects of all kinds, and the fitful nights of sleep on snake infested ground." The Light Guard did so well in these exercises that a number of its members were chosen to take part in maneuvers that occurred in North and South Carolina later that year.[21]

On 5 December 1941 these men returned from the Carolinas to Camp Livingston after an exhausting but successful experience, but they were not allowed an extended period of relaxation. For on the morning of Sunday 7 December, without the formality of a declaration of war, the forces of Imperial Japan carried out a surprise attack against the United States fleet and the military installa-tions at Pearl Harbor in Hawaii. The next day President Roosevelt, eloquently denouncing "the day that will live in infamy," secured a declaration of war from Congress against the aggressors from the Far East. Nazi Germany and Fascist Italy rallied to the side of Japan, and the United States found itself in the middle of World War II.[22]

It is in such a situation as this that Americans are especially indebted to the historic traditions of the militia that have lived on in the twentieth-century National Guard. The citizen-soldiers had in peacetime preserved both the military skills so badly needed in wartime and the ability to transmit this knowledge to new recruits by maintaining a nucleus of individuals who could teach in training camps. In this way the guardsmen played a vital role in America's speedy effort to create an army to meet its security requirements in the perilous conditions that existed at the end of 1941. Overall War Department policy created a situation in which the Light Guard's proud traditions continued in World War II, not by the unit's going to war as a group but by its useful and constructive role in providing leadership and preparation for recruits from a wide variety of backgrounds. On 8 December, while Americans within and outside of the armed forces were recovering from the numbing shock of Pearl Harbor, the 125th Infantry was "relieved . . . from assignment to [the] 32d Division" and consequently did not accompany the latter to New Guinea. This separation for the Detroiters was a result of the policy that the army had begun implementing at the end of the 1930s, when it went from a square to a triangular organization for divisions, that is to say, from four to three regiments for each unit. Ironically, this change at the beginning of

World War II separated the Light Guardsmen from the group with which they had shared such a dramatic and important history during World War I.[23]

Yet the Detroit militia carried on its long-standing reputation for excellence both by providing highly professional training for fellow soldiers and by contributing so many of its members to serve in combat in other units during the war, in particular with the remainder of the Thirty-second Division. Within this unit Headquarters Company of the Second Battalion received battle honors known as silver bands for New Guinea, Leyte, and Luzon, while Company H was awarded silver bands for Papua, New Guinea, Leyte, and Luzon. Company H was also accorded a "Distinguished Unit Streamer" for Papua. Companies B and C of the First Battalion are recognized as "entitled to: World War II-AP: Aleutian Islands Campaign Participation Credit." The members of the 225th Infantry, the present embodiment of the Light Guard, are especially proud of these campaigns.[24]

When the news of the attack on Hawaii reached the men of the 125th, they knew they would soon be departing from Camp Livingston. Their original year's duty had already been extended, but in the atmosphere of wartime secrecy no one knew their destination. As one source describes the situation, "It was not until December 11, 1941 that the Regiment boarded the trains under sealed orders. Would it be California? Hawaii? The Phillipines [sic]? No one knew, and all had their own ideas." Journeying over the impressive reaches of Arizona, "the tired men thought the West a long desert until they sighted the mountains in the region of San Bernardino, California," according to another source. The regiment's first stop

proved to be Pomona, where it camped at the Los Angeles County Fairgrounds. The 125th became the reserve for the Army's southern California sector. Its commander there, General Joseph W. Stilwell, became during the course of the war one of the most famous, colorful, and controversial American military commanders in Asia.[25]

The regiment stayed at the Los Angeles Fairgrounds for forty-eight hours and was then sent to the Santa Anita Race Track. One account of this period noted that "although there were no races before wildly cheering and wildly betting crowds, Whirlaway, champion money winner of all time, put on early morning shows for the Infantry with fast workouts around the famous track." After another two days the Detroiters again moved on, but this time they were sent in different directions: "Regimental Headquarters and the Second Battalion set up a C[ommand] P[ost] at the Los Angeles Municipal Airport, the First Battalion moved to the oil rich and wide awake Long Beach area, and the Third Battalion shifted to Burbank." These assignments were of vital importance because of the great concern about the possibility of sabotage of key industries and installations in the early days of the American participation in the war. The country's leadership was aware that such tactics had been practiced by the enemy in fighting against other nations. Among the responsibilities the 125th assumed at this time was the establishment of the first significant army protection of the crucial aircraft industry of southern California.[26]

The 125th, however, performed these duties for a short period only. By Christmas 1941 the regiment was scattered to locations in three states. Regimental headquarters was established in a desert area in Needles, California, and the First Battalion took up a position at Flagstaff, Arizona, having responsibility for the security of the bridges and tunnels of the Santa Fe Railroad in that state as well as of Coolidge Dam. The Second Battalion, stationed at Camp Siebert in Nevada, maintained a watch over Boulder Dam. Other units of the 125th assumed tasks at various places in Arizona and California.[27]

Continual moving became a way of life for the Light Guardsmen. The regiment was briefly located in Griffith Park in Los Angeles early in January 1942. Later in the month "the Third Battalion returned to Burbank, California." Perhaps the most notable activity of the 125th during this period involved the making of "several training films of tactics of small Infantry units under the direction of well known Hollywood Producers." In addition to its continual postings to various tasks and locations where it was needed, the regiment had by March 1942 furnished many of its members both to other groups and to Officer Candidate School. To fill its ranks the 125th received recruits from various western states and established a training center near Santa Barbara, California.[28]

In April 1942 the regiment became part of the Northern California Sector of the Western Defense Command. For this assignment, headquarters was at Gilroy, California. The line of coastal defense posts assumed by the 125th stretched a distance of 250 miles from San Francisco to Camp Cook. The notable places guarded included San Jose, Monterey, Palo Alto, and Fresno. By 1943 the circumstances of the war in the Pacific had so improved that the chances of a Japanese invasion of the United States were substantially lessened. At

this point the Light Guard regiment was relieved of its coastal defense duty and ordered to Fort Ord near Monterey, where the members of the unit presumed that they would get ready for overseas duty. They assumed Alaska would be the destination of the 125th. After rapid preparations involving working around the clock, "the task of equipping and packing was completed in half the time usually devoted to such a large job, and on September 28, 1943 two full trains had been loaded and made ready to move when orders arrived that the entire move had been cancelled." After disembarking the men began an intensive course at Fort Ord and then in October returned to their former assignment of guarding the California coast. When patrolling these rounds once again, some of the Light Guardsmen must have pondered on the nature of military bureaucracy in a time of war.[29]

The 125th continued in its assignment on the shores of the Pacific until February 1944, when it was transferred to Camp Maxey, Texas. At that time the regiment became part of the Twenty-third Corps, Fourth Army. The Light Guard's task became, in the "words of the letter from the Headquarters of the Army Ground Forces, 'the retraining of enlisted men of various arms and services as Infantry Replacements.'" Throughout this period of continual travel, reassignments, reposting, and shifting—no doubt frustrating for those who hoped to go overseas—the Detroiters had performed the vital function of guarding domestic facilities essential to the war effort. Many individual members of the organization carried on the legacy of the Light Guard by entering other units. As a result, a good many of the original Light Guardsmen had been drained off, and "soon there was nothing but a scant cadre left of the old Regiment, but it was being filled at the same time with men from all branches of the services who were to be transformed into infantrymen."[30]

Individuals who had not initially been part of the Light Guard entered the unit in great numbers during the war, but the core of leadership remaining from the old 125th did much to inculcate the standards, traditions, and martial skills of Detroit's senior militia group in a myriad of young Americans from all sections of the country. This process provided an important service for the army as the war approached its height. When the recruits readied by the regiment "finished their training, [they] went immediately to replacement depots to fill the depleted ranks of the fighting units overseas."[31]

Although the remaining cadre of the 125th might have preferred to have been in combat, its members understood their duties as soldiers. They conducted in a disciplined fashion the intensive preparation of infantrymen so urgently needed by United States forces during this crucial period. It was perhaps symbolic that soon after D-day, the occasion of the Normandy landing of allied forces in Europe, the Light Guard in Texas received a letter from the commanding general of the Ninety-ninth Division commending the guard's high level of performance in a recent Infantry Day Parade. Quality on the drill field prepared the way for achievement on the battlefield.[32]

On 10 December 1944 the regiment was moved to Camp Gruber, Oklahoma, where it served in the Thirty-sixth Corps, Fourth Army. Finally in late February 1945 the soldiers of the 125th journeyed "to Camp Rucker, Alabama, where they were assigned to the Replacement & School Command and attached to [the] Infantry Replacement Training Center." Throughout the spring and summer members of the regiment were engaged either in preparing troops for combat or in processing for overseas duty individuals who had originally been sent to Camp Rucker for advanced training but who, "due to the urgent need in the European Theater for" manpower, were at once sent abroad without additional military education. The war in Europe ended in May 1945, and Japan ceased hostilities in August 1945. Consequently, "the War Department decided to inactivate the Regiment and return it to its original status as a unit of the Michigan National Guard." The actual date on which this took place was 20 September 1945. The 125th had been summoned into federal service for one year in the fall of 1941; when its members left the United States Army their tour of duty was twenty-five days short of lasting five years.[33]

Following World War II, the 125th underwent many changes, but the Light Guard retained its unique character. On 26 November 1946 the 125th was expanded, redesignated the 425th, and assigned to the Forty-sixth Infantry Division. Then on 15 March 1959 it became the 225th Infantry, the First Battle Group of the same division. Finally on 15 March 1963 the unit was named the First Battalion, 225th Infantry. By permission of the Department of Defense, the official designation of the organization is the Detroit Light Guard, First Battalion, 225th Infantry. It is one of the few National Guard units allowed to retain its original name in honor of its distinctive past. In the space age the history of the Light Guard provides a source of strength and professionalism for men and officers who must cope with the complexities and challenges of modern warfare.[34]

The Light Guard continued its work as Detroit's senior militia organization and its support of the city as a whole. This was amply demonstrated by the building of the Light Guard Armory on East Eight Mile Road. The guard's Brush Street Armory was destroyed in a fire on 17 April 1945. As a result the group had to relocate into a converted automobile factory at 285 Piquette Avenue, where it still remained when Lieutenant Colonel Ford D. McParland assumed command of the 425th in 1951. McParland decided to build a new armory, and his accomplishments illustrate the best in the Light Guard's tradition of leadership in the community as well as in things military.[35]

A lieutenant colonel when he took charge of the regiment on 1 December 1951, McParland was promoted to full colonel in March 1952 and headed the unit until his retirement from active duty in January 1960. Even by the standards of the Light Guard he was an unusually dedicated officer who devoted all his energies to the group and who seemed to have no other avocation. Colonel McParland focused his efforts on expanding the unit's program of activities, preserving the legacy of "Detroit's Own" militia, informing both the membership and the general public about the Light Guard, and leading the endeavors that culminated in the building of the present armory.[36]

An officer with a particularly strong sense of history, this commander lost no opportunity to impress the distinctive and distinguished past of his group of citizen-soldiers on Detroiters. He did this because he felt the people should know about this valuable resource of their city as well as to mobilize the public support necessary to insure the building of the new armory he felt the 425th required to carry on its mission. Colonel McParland concentrated on achieving his program with a single-mindedness that might have seemed almost zealotry to unsympathetic observers, and he did not fear to offend influential individuals in reaching his goals. Everything he did was to fulfill the needs of the Light Guard. This leader's devotion and satisfactions came from what seems in retrospect to have been a high degree of identification with his regiment, its traditions, its responsibilities, and its future.[37]

Despite its limited financial resources in the 1950s, under the new commander's persistent and untiring leadership the Light Guard sponsored the "best 'Military Balls' held in the City of Detroit." Colonel McParland was responsible for organizing an officer's mess, a post exchange, and a bagpipe band. He also revived two neglected traditions from the militia's past: a women's auxiliary and a military band. The fact that some of these accomplishments disappeared after the end of McParland's unusually energetic stewardship of the regiment should not obscure his achievements. His attention to the history of "Detroit's Own" was illustrated by his assignments to junior officers to conduct research on the topic. The colonel also wrote letters to community leaders about the organization's past.[38]

Of all the accomplishments of this intrepid man none matched the importance or the historical appropriateness of his success in heading the drive to build the new Light Guard Armory. The essence of Detroit's senior militia company had always been a distinctive blend of military duty and community responsibility. This laudable synthesis was embodied in the campaign to construct a new home for the 425th. The structure would not only enable the unit to carry out its National Guard duties in the increasingly perilous age of the atomic bomb and the cold war but would also serve a wide variety of civic purposes for metropolitan Detroit. McParland's own words, which perhaps reflect the candor and simplicity of style of an earlier generation, nonetheless eloquently reflect the spirit behind the colonel's chief aim and most significant accomplishment:

> This goal is more regimental than personal because the Commanders have come and gone over a period of 123 years. Only the regiment is permanent and a part of Detroit, in fact it is Detroit. It's [sic] place is second as an organization only to the Detroit Fire Department in services to this city, churches excluded. . . .
>
> We are simply citizen soldiers of Detroit from all conceiveable [sic] walks of life, who turn from our workaday pursuits to train as soldiers to be ready when the City or Nation calls. Non-Sectarian, Non-Racial, Non-Partisan, your civic military force.[39]

The scope and quality of the proposed armory required not only aid from local, state, and federal governments but private contributions as well. To mobilize the necessary support for the project McParland formed in March 1953 a citizens' committee that focused on raising funds for the building. Walker Cisler, president of the Detroi

Edison Company, served as the committee's general chairman, and Henry J. Sullivan, one of Cisler's assistants at Edison, was especially active in the group. A wide variety of individuals prominent in the civic and commercial life of the metropolitan area were members, including Colonel McParland and Lieutenant Colonel James F. Clark, representing the 425th Infantry.[40]

The work of the committee in combination with the efforts of McParland and other members of the 425th produced success. The Detroit Light Guard Armory, when complete, was the largest that had been constructed in the United States after World War II. It cost approximately $3 million, nearly $600 thousand of which was provided in cash, property, and services by the city of Detroit, $200 thousand by Wayne County, nearly $245 thousand by the state of Michigan, and the remainder by the federal government. The citizens' committee raised a total of $138 thousand to pay for the furnishings. This was necessary because regulations of the Department of the Army, the branch of the national government that made funds from that level available to the 425th, prohibited using its money for outfitting the armory. The sums for a myriad of items ranging from lockers to office furniture had to be privately provided. The Detroit Armory Corporation, the supportive organization of the Detroit Light Guard, also contributed a considerable amount toward the heavy expense of equipping its new home.[41]

The ground breaking for the building took place on 4 June 1956 in a simple and brief ceremony presided over by Colonel McParland, marking the first step toward constructing the headquarters for the Light Guard at Farwell Field on East

Eight Mile Road. More dramatic and elaborate was the laying of the cornerstone for the structure on 14 December of that year. The featured speaker on this occasion was the secretary of the army, Wilber M. Brucker. He was a particularly appropriate orator because he was not only a former governor of Michigan but had also been a member of the Thirty-second Division. Lieutenant Colonel James F. Clark served as both narrator of the program and master of ceremonies. The many notables present included Governor G. Mennen Williams of Michigan, Acting Mayor Louis C. Miriani of Detroit, and Major General Gordon A. MacDonald, the commander of the Forty-sixth Infantry Division.[42]

In September 1957, the new building was in condition for some units of the regiment to begin moving in, but the official dedication did not take place until later. Detroit's senior militia company had found a home, and the metropolitan area had a structure that could be utilized for a large variety of functions, such as shows and exhibits of widespread community interest, school commencements, and dinners and celebrations of unions and fraternal and religious organizations.[43]

One local newspaper commented that the new armory would represent a "dream come true" for Ford D. McParland, who had worked so diligently for it, but the same could have been said for the many other members of the 425th and their friends in the community who had supported them. But certainly without the tenacious leadership of that capable regimental commander, success might have eluded the guards, and the results very much embodied the outlines of McParland's aims for the building. He was understandably proud of the "30,000-square-foot drill floor . . . and the modern maintenance-and-repair shop in the basement

for the unit's rolling stock." The generous facilities included sufficient space so that each company could have "its own area, offices, assembly room and arms vault." Training facilities included not only a rifle range but also "one of the most important considerations in the planning . . . locker room facilities, ample to allow 1,450 guardsmen to shower and change back to civilian clothes without lining up for the privilege as the units" expanded. Particularly reassuring were the vaults in which the armaments of the organization would be kept. They were "14 inches thick, with burglar proof locks." Indeed, so imposing were these security areas that they were equipped with "panic buttons" so that no individuals would accidentally be locked inside of them.[44]

From all points of view then, from the new armory's capability for military training to its potential for civic functions, the 425th Infantry and its commander had every reason to be proud of their accomplishment. The general public as well as distinguished leaders were invited to the official dedication and opening of the new Light Guard Armory on 16 November 1957. The activities of the evening symbolized beautifully the heritage of the town founded by Cadillac as not only a trading center for the French but one which combined Gallic cultural and military influence.[45]

Appropriately, the dedication took place on the anniversary of the exact date on which Detroit's senior militia group had been reorganized under the name Light Guard in 1855. The official program began at 7:30 P.M., with music provided by the bands of not only the 139th Michigan National Guard but also of the Thirty-second, Red Arrow Division, of which the Light Guard had been a unit during a period of some of its most notable service. Clergymen representing the Protestant, Roman Catholic, and Jewish faiths participated in the ceremony. Governor Williams, once again attending a Light Guard function, and Councilman Eugene I. Van Antwerp, representing the acting mayor of Detroit, Louis C. Miriani, were among the many notables present. At 8:15 tours of the facility commenced, and at 9:00 dancing began.[46]

Colonel McParland was so committed to the important functions the Detroit Light Guard Armory housed that he served as the building's full-time manager from 1957 until the end of 1961, continuing in that role a year after he had retired from active duty with the Michigan National Guard. In February 1960 he had been promoted to brigadier general in that organization. In 1963 McParland died in California, but his funeral and burial took place in Detroit. Symbolically and appropriately, the "hearse carrying his body did pause for a moment in front of the armory as it proceeded to the cemetery."[47]

Since World War II the Light Guard, whether as the 125th, the 425th, or the 225th Infantry of the Michigan National Guard, has continued to maintain its tradition of service and excellence in an often perilous world. During the Korean War the Forty-sixth Division was one of ten National Guard units placed on alert by the army, although it was not called into duty for that struggle. During the Detroit riots of 1967 the 225th was summoned into federal service from 24 July until 2 August and aided regular units of the United States Army in restoring stability to the city during that confused and tragic period. In the 1970s and 1980s the 225th has continued to stand on guard for the metropolitan area in peace and war. The connection between the local organization of citizen-soldiers and the United States Army is well illustrated not only by the Detroit Light Guard's official title of the First Battalion, 225th Infantry of the Michigan National Guard, but also by the personal involvement of such individuals as Colonel George Stapleton, Jr., who was the son of a former commander of the 425th, served in that unit himself, won an appointment to the United States Military Academy at West Point, and became an officer in the regular army. The Light Guard carries on today in the tradition of the principles of George Washington, the first commander in chief under the nation's present constitution. The father of our country spoke of the importance of maintaining a well-trained militia that could act in times of either local need or national danger.[48] "Detroit's Own," the Detroit Light Guard with its roots in history going back to the early French and British citizen-soldiers in this area, still proudly serves under the tiger's head emblem and embodies the standards of its motto,

"Deo Libertati Gloriae."

Notes

1. United States Department of the Army, *Lineage and Honors.*

2. Robert H. Ferrell, *American Diplomacy: A History,* rev. and expanded ed. (New York, 1969), 562–75.

3. Memorandum on the Founding of the Old Detroit Light Guard, n.d., Storer.

4. *Detroit News,* 20 Nov. 1929.

5. Ibid.

6. R. S. Gehlert to Robert E. Mason, 10 Dec. 1928; Mason to A. S. Hampton, 11 Dec. 1928; Hampton to Mason, 14 Dec. 1928, DAC.

7. *Detroit Free Press,* 9 Nov. 1930; *Detroit News,* 16 Nov. 1930.

8. Alexander DeConde, *A History of American Foreign Policy,* 3d ed. (New York, 1978), 2:139–49; Daniel M. Smith, *The American Diplomatic Experience* (Boston, 1972), 355–64.

9. Smith, 338–40; DeConde, 2:150–55.

10. DeConde, 2:156–61; Smith, 362–69.

11. Mahon, 180–82.

12. Ibid., 178.

13. Sidney Fine, *Sit-Down: The General Motors Strike of 1936–1937* (Ann Arbor, Mich., 1969), 144, 236.

14. Ibid., 242.

15. Ibid., 243.

16. Ibid., 247, 319. For an overview of the Flint strike, see also Sidney Fine, "The General Motors Sit-Down Strike: A Re-examination," *American Historical Review* 70 (Apr. 1965): 691–713.

17. "Your History!" 4.

18. *Let the Drum Beat: 125th Infantry, Its History during the First Year of World War II,* n.p., n.d.; Lieutenant Colonel John D. McDaniels to Detroit Armory Corporation History Committee, [Apr. 1981], DAC.

19. McDaniels, "One Twenty-Fifth Infantry: Golden Anniversary of Its Organization in World War I and Silver Anniversary of Its Participation in World War II," 3, DAC, typescript; Colonel Louis P. Labbe, "Historical Notes: 125th Infantry," Camp Rucker, Ala., 20 Sept. 1945, 13, DAC, mimeo.

20. Labbe, 13, DAC; McDaniels, 3, DAC; *Let the Drum Beat,* 9.

21. Labbe, 13–14, DAC; *Let the Drum Beat,* 9; McDaniels, 3, DAC.

22. Labbe, 14, DAC: *Let the Drum Beat,* 9; McDaniels, 3, DAC; Ferrell, 628–30.

23. Lieutenant Colonel James F. Clark, interview with author, Detroit, 12 June 1986; United States Department of the Army, *Lineage and Honors;* Mahon, 178–85.

24. "History of 425th Infantry Regt.," Colonel Ford D. McParland Papers, DAC, Photocopy; United States Department of the Army, *Lineage and Honors;* United States War Department, *Units Entitled to Battle Credits,* General Orders no. 12, 1 Feb. 1945 (Washington, 1945), 26, 31, 35, 110, 113; United States Department of the Army, *Units Entitled to Battle Credits,* General Orders no. 29, 21 Apr. 1948 (Washington, 1948), 1, 4; United States Department of the Army, *Unit Citation and Campaign Participation Credit Register,* Pam 672–1 (Washington, 1961), 68; Clark to author, 5 May 1987.

25. Labbe, 14–15, DAC; *Let the Drum Beat,* 11.

26. Labbe, 15, DAC; *Let the Drum Beat,* 11.

27. *Let the Drum Beat,* 11; Labbe, 15, DAC.

28. Labbe, 15–16, DAC.

29. Ibid., 16.

30. Ibid., 16–17.

31. Ibid., 17.

32. Ibid.

33. Ibid., 17–18; Ferrell, 660–61.

34. United States Department of the Army, *Lineage and Honors;* Captain Alan A. Redner, interview with author, Detroit, 25 May 1986.

35. Milo M. Quaife, *This Is Detroit, 1701–1951: Two Hundred and Fifty Years in Pictures,* ed. William

White (Detroit, 1951), 58; Clark, interview, 12 June 1986.

36. Chief Warrant Officer 4 Alfred Wyborski to author, 18 June 1986, DAC; Ford D. McParland, document urging Detroit officials to support drive for new armory, 13 Oct. 1953, viii–ix, McParland Papers, DAC.

37. Wyborski to author, 18 June 1986, DAC; Clark, interview, 12 June 1986.

38. Wyborski to author, 18 June 1986; Lieutenant Robert L. Thomas to McParland, 23 Mar. 1954, McParland Papers, DAC; McParland, document, 13 Oct. 1953, ii–vi, McParland Papers, ibid.

39. McParland, document, 13 Oct. 1953, ii, McParland Papers, DAC.

40. Clark to author, 12 June 1986, DAC; Wyborski to author, 18 June 1986, DAC; McParland, document, 13 Oct. 1953, vi, McParland Papers, DAC; Donald S. Kiskadden, "New Light Guard Armory Is Yours—Needs Your Help," *The Detroiter* 47 (11 Mar. 1957): 6.

41. Clark to author, 12 June 1986, DAC; Clark, interview, 12 June 1986; *Detroit Times,* 11 Aug. 1957; Kiskadden, 6.

42. Clark to author, 12 June 1986, DAC; Clark, interview, 12 June 1986; *Detroit News,* 5 June 1956; "Official Souvenir Program for the Ground Breaking Ceremony for the Light Guard Armory," 4 June 1956, Scrapbook, DAC; *Detroit News,* 15 Dec. 1956; *Detroit Times,* 15 Dec. 1956; "Program. Cornerstone Laying of the 'Light Guard Armory,'" Scrapbook, DAC.

43. Clark to author, 12 June 1986, DAC; Clark, interview, 12 June 1986; *Legal Advertiser* (Detroit), 14 Nov. 1957; *Grand River Star* (Detroit), 29 Mar. 1957; *Detroit Times,* 11 Aug. 1957.

44. *Detroit Times,* 11 Aug. 1957.

45. *Legal Advertiser* (Detroit), 14 Nov. 1957; *East Sider* (Detroit), 14 Nov. 1957.

46. *Legal Advertiser* (Detroit), 14 Nov. 1957; *East Sider* (Detroit), 14 Nov. 1957.

47. Wyborski to author, 18 June 1986, DAC; Special Order no. 36, Ronald D. McDonald, adjutant general of Michigan, 20 Feb. 1960, DAC; Wyborski, interview with author, Detroit, 26 May 1987.

48. Clark to author, 12 June 1986, DAC; Clark, interview, 12 June 1986; United States Department of the Army, *Lineage and Honors;* Clark to author, 22 Sept. 1986, DAC; Russell F. Weigley, *History of the United States Army,* enl. ed. (Bloomington, Ind., 1984), 80.

BIBLIOGRAPHY

Alger, R. A. *The Spanish-American War.* New York, 1901.

Bald, F. Clever. *Detroit's First American Decade, 1796 to 1805.* University of Michigan Publications, History and Political Science. Vol. 16. Ann Arbor, Mich., 1948.

_____. *Michigan in Four Centuries.* New York, 1954.

Bates, George C. "Reminiscences of the Brady Guards." *Historical Collections: Collections and Researches Made by the Michigan Pioneer and Historical Society* 13 (1888): 530–46.

Brady, Hugh. "General Hugh Brady: A Biographical Sketch of General Hugh Brady, by Himself." *Pioneer Collections: Report of the Pioneer Society of the State of Michigan* 3 (1881): 84–87.

_____. "Reports of General Brady on the Patriot War." *Canadian Historical Review* 31 (Mar. 1950): 56–68.

Brundage, Lyle D. "The Organization, Administration, and Training of the United States Ordinary and Volunteer Militia, 1792–1861." Ed.D. diss., University of Michigan, 1958.

"Cadillac Papers." *Historical Collections: Collections and Researches Made by the Michigan Pioneer and Historical Society* 33 (1904): 36–715.

Catton, Bruce. *The American Heritage Short History of the Civil War.* New York, 1963.

Charnley, Jeffrey G. "'Neglected Honor,' The Life of General A. S. Williams of Michigan (1810–1878)." Ph.D. diss., Michigan State University, 1983.

Clowes, Walter F. *The Detroit Light Guard: A Complete Record of This Organization from Its Foundation to the Present Day.* Detroit, 1900.

Cosmas, Graham A. *An Army for Empire: The United States Army in the Spanish-American War.* Columbia, Mo., 1971.

DeConde, Alexander. *A History of American Foreign Policy.* 3d ed. Vol. 2. New York, 1978.

Detroit Public Library. *Detroit in Its World Setting.* Detroit, 1953.

Dierks, Jack C. *A Leap to Arms: The Cuban Campaign of 1898.* Philadelphia, 1970.

Dunbar, Willis F. *Michigan: A History of the Wolverine State.* Rev. ed. George S. May. Grand Rapids, Mich., 1980.

Ellis, Helen H., comp. *Michigan in the Civil War: A Guide to the Material in Detroit Newspapers 1861–1866.* Lansing, Mich., 1965.

Farmer, Silas. *History of Detroit and Wayne County and Early Michigan.* 3d ed., rev. and enl. 1890. Reprint. Detroit, 1969.

Ferrell, Robert H. *American Diplomacy: A History.* Rev. and expanded ed. New York, 1969.

Fine, Sidney. *Sit-Down; The General Motors Strike of 1936–1937.* Ann Arbor, Mich., 1969.

Fuller, George N., ed. *Michigan: A Centennial History of the State and Its People.* Vol. 1. Chicago, 1939.

Gilpin, Alex R. *The Territory of Michigan [1805–1837].* East Lansing, Mich., 1970.

————. *The War of 1812 in the Old Northwest.* 1958. Reprint. East Lansing, Mich., 1968.

Isham, Frederic S., and Purcell and Hogan, comps. *History of the Detroit Light Guard: Its Records and Achievements.* Detroit, 1896.

Joint War History Commissions of Michigan and Wisconsin. *The 32nd Division in the World War, 1917–1919.* Madison, Wis., 1920.

Kiskadden, Donald S. "New Light Guard Armory Is Yours—Needs Your Help." *The Detroiter* 47 (11 Mar. 1957): 6.

Leech, Margaret, and Harry J. Brown. *The Garfield Orbit.* New York, 1978.

Let the Drum Beat: 125th Infantry, Its History during the First Year of World War II. N.p., n.d.

Link, Arthur S. *Woodrow Wilson and the Progressive Era, 1910–1917.* New York, 1954.

McLaughlin, Doris B. *Michigan Labor: A Brief History from 1818 to the Present.* Ann Arbor, Mich., 1970.

McPherson, James M. *Ordeal by Fire: The Civil War and Reconstruction.* New York, 1982.

Mahon, John K. *History of the Militia and the National Guard.* New York, 1983.

May, Ernest R. *Imperial Democracy: The Emergence of America as a Great Power.* New York, 1961.

May, George S. *Michigan and the Civil War Years, 1860–1866: A Wartime Chronicle.* Lansing, Mich., 1964.

O'Toole, G. J. A. *The Spanish War, An American Epic—1898.* New York, 1984.

Palmer, John M. *America in Arms.* 1941. Reprint. New York, 1979.

Peckham, Howard H. *Pontiac and the Indian Uprising.* Princeton, N.J., 1947.

Quaife, Milo M. *This Is Detroit, 1701–1951: Two Hundred and Fifty Years in Pictures.* Ed. William White. Detroit, 1951.

————, and Sidney Glazer, *Michigan: From Primitive Wilderness to Industrial Commonwealth.* New York, 1948.

Randall, J. G., and David Donald. *The Civil War and Reconstruction.* 2d ed. Boston, 1961.

Robertson, John. "Brief Military History of Michigan as a Territory and as a State." In Michigan Commission for the Semi-Centennial of the Admission of the State of Michigan into the Union. *Addresses Delivered at Its Celebration, June 15, 1886,* 433–510. Detroit, 1886.

————. *Michigan in the War.* Lansing, Mich., 1882.

Ross, Robert B. *Early Bench and Bar of Detroit.* Detroit, 1907.

_____. *Landmarks of Detroit.* Detroit, 1898.

Rutman, Darrett B. *A Militant New World, 1607–1640.* 1959. Reprint. New York, 1979.

Smith, Daniel M. *The American Diplomatic Experience.* Boston, 1972.

Stokesbury, James L. *A Short History of World War I.* New York, 1981.

Stone, Richard G., Jr. *A Brittle Sword: The Kentucky Militia, 1776–1912.* Lexington, Ky., 1977.

Thomas, Benjamin P. *Abraham Lincoln: A Biography.* New York, 1952.

Trask, David F. *The War with Spain in 1898.* New York, 1981.

United States Department of the Army. *Lineage and Honors: 225th Infantry (Detroit Light Guard).* Washington, 1969.

_____. *Unit Citation and Campaign Participation Credit Register.* Pam 672–1. Washington, 1961.

_____. *Units Entitled to Battle Credits.* General Orders no. 29, 21 Apr. 1948. Washington, 1948.

United States War Department. *Units Entitled to Battle Credits.* General Orders no. 12, 1 Feb. 1945. Washington, 1945.

Utley, Henry M. *Michigan as a State, from the Close of the Civil War to the End of the Nineteenth Century.* Vol. 4 of Utley and Byron M. Cutcheon, *Michigan as a Province, Territory and State, the Twenty-Sixth Member of the Federal Union.* New York, 1906.

Weigley, Russell F. *History of the United States Army.* Enl. ed. Bloomington, Ind., 1984.

Woodford, Frank B. *Father Abraham's Children: Michigan Episodes in the Civil War.* Detroit, 1961.

"Your History!" *The Light Guard* 1 (6 May 1952): 1, 4.

Zackem, Matilde Z. "Michigan's Aid in the Black Hawk War." Master's thesis, Wayne State University, 1943.

Manuscripts

Burton Historical Collection, Detroit Public Library. (BHC)

    Brady Guards Papers.

    Detroit Light Guard Minutes.

    Detroit Light Guard Veteran Corps Selections.

    Detroit Light Infantry Minutes.

    Palmer, Friend. Scrapbooks of Miscellaneous Items.

    Williams, Alpheus S. Papers.

    Woodbridge, William. Papers.

    Woodward, Augustus B. Papers.

Detroit Armory Corporation. (DAC)

    Labbe, Louis P. "Historical Notes: 125th Infantry." Camp Rucker, Ala., 20 Sept. 1945. Mimeo.

    Letters.

    McDaniels, John D. "One Twenty-Fifth Infantry: Golden Anniversary of Its Organization in World War I and Silver Anniversary of Its Participation in World War II." Typescript.

    McParland, Ford D. Papers.

    Scrapbooks.

Special Order no. 36, Ronald D. McDonald, Adjutant General of Michigan, 20 Feb. 1960.

Tanglefoot, Corporal [pseud.]. Diary. Typescript.

Michigan State Archives, Lansing. (MSA)

   Records of the Michigan Military Establishment.

Records Relating to the Black Hawk War.

Storer, Frank E.

   Memorandum on the Founding of the Old Detroit Light Guard.

   Minutes of the Grayson Light Guards.

Newspapers

Cleveland Herald Leader.

Detroit Daily Advertiser.

Detroit Daily Tribune.

Detroit Evening News.

Detroit Evening Telegraph.

Detroit Free Press.

Detroit Gazette.

Detroit Journal.

Detroit News.

Detroit Saturday Night.

Detroit Times.

Detroit Tribune.

East Sider (Detroit).

Grand River Star (Detroit).

Legal Advertiser (Detroit).

#

165

Stanley D. Solvick teaches history at Wayne State University. He received his B.A., M.A., and Ph.D. from the University of Michigan. He has published numerous articles on William Howard Taft and American politics in scholarly journals.

The manuscript was edited by Anne M. G. Adamus. The book was designed by Don Ross. The typeface for the text is Goudy Old Style. The display faces are Profil and Goudy Old Style. This book is printed on 70-lb. Sterling Litho Matte and is bound in Holliston Mills' Roxite Vellum.

Manufactured in the United States of America.